Whispers in the Willows

Who killed Rebekah Gould?

Who killed Amanda Tusing?

Who killed Karen Johnson Swift?

And why?

George Jared

Groves-Holliman Publishers

Groves-Holliman Publishers

Copyright © 2019 by Groves-Holliman Publishers LLC.

All rights reserved. No part of this publication may be reproduced or transmitted in any form or by any means without the expressed written consent from Groves-Holliman Publishers or as expressed by law. This includes, but is not limited to, electronic forms of communication, photocopying, recording, or by any information storage and retrieval system.

About the author ...

Award winning journalist and best-selling true crime author George Jared takes readers on a harrowing journey into the depths of heinous murders he's covered during his career.

Whispers in the Willows chronicles the unsolved murders of 22-year-old Rebekah Gould, 20-year-old Amanda Tusing and a mother of four, Karen Johnson Swift. There are chapters dedicated to his coverage of four executions on Death Row in April, 2017. The book ends with two chapters about a different kind of murder story, those told by holocaust survivors Henry Greenbaum and Estelle Laughlin.

Amanda Tusing parted ways with her fiancée on a rain soaked night to stay the night at her parents' house. A little more than an hour after she left, the young woman's body was floating lifeless in a waterway. During the last two weeks of April, the state of Arkansas tried to execute eight Death Row inmates before its supply of death drugs went out of date. The crimes committed by these men cannot be imagined. Karen Johnson Swift, a mother of four, vanished without a trace. Who killed her and why? Two holocaust survivors gave gripping and powerful stories about watching loved ones murdered at the hands of Nazi soldiers.

The last chapter is about the ongoing unsolved Rebekah Gould murder case. It's been nearly 15 years and powerful new evidence has surfaced, but one question remains. Will the police make an arrest in a case that seems like it should be relatively easy to solve?

Whispers is the third true crime book written by Mr. Jared.

The Creek Side Bones chronicled the brutal slayings of a family of four, a teenage beauty queen, and a mother who vanished while on a walk down a country road. The book also covers a prominent attorney and judge who descended into murder and madness. It also contains an update on a 13-year-old unsolved murder case.

A knock at the door on a rainy, windy night ended Carl Elliott's life and soon after his wife, Lisa, and son, Gregory were also murdered. What happened to his little girl, Felicia, is hard to contemplate. Sidney Nicole Randall went to bed one night and vanished. Her fate is hard to grasp. Bridgett Sellers went for a walk one day and disappeared. Where she was found and how she got there is hard to believe. Bob Castleman was one of the most respected men in his hometown until drugs, thefts, and even a murder consumed him. Rebekah Gould's killers are still free even though many in the law enforcement community know who took the 22-year-old's life.

Mr. Jared's first book, *Witches in West Memphis,* provided an insider's view into one of the notorious murder cases in U.S. legal history. *Witches* chronicled the plight of Damien Echols, Jason Baldwin, and Jessie Misskelley Jr., three men from Marion, Ark., convicted in the 1993 slayings of thee eight-year-old boys in West Memphis. The men, dubbed "The West Memphis Three" spent more than 18 years in prison before they were released after enormous national and international pressure. Mr. Jared wrote more stories about the WM3 case than any other journalist in the world.

Filmmakers Joe Berlinger and Bruce Sinofsky, the famed directors of the *Paradise Lost* franchise that exposed the case, have interviewed him more than once, as has *West of Memphis* Director Amy Berg. National Public Radio has interviewed the journalist, and numerous other news agencies around the country have sought his insights.

Mr. Jared has spent more than a decade writing award winning stories for publications throughout Northeast Arkansas. He's covered capital murder cases, politics, catastrophic weather events, and other newsmakers. He's won coveted accolades with the Associated Press Managing Editors and the Arkansas Press Association, consistently beating reporters from the vaunted *Arkansas Democrat Gazette*. He's won 11 first place awards for news, beat reporting, feature writing, investigative reporting, and others.

The long-time newsman resides in Northeast Arkansas with his wife and children.

He's been cited as a source in the Academy Award nominated film, *Paradise Lost Three: Purgatory,* the *New York Times* best-seller *Life After Death* written by Damien Echols and the book *Untying the Knot* by John Mark Byers and Greg Day. Jared was also featured in the hit podcast *Hell and Gone* that chronicled the Gould's murder.

Editor's Note: Several of the cases outlined in the following chapters contain information that was derived from anonymous sources. Mr. Jared has always preferred to use on the record sources for news stories and his true crime books, but in these cold, unsolved cases, many detectives and other law officers are not free to speak on the record. Limited liberties were taken with sensitive information. The end goal is to provide the reader with as much information as possible.

Table of Contents

Chapter One – Amanda "Mandy" Tusing

Chapter Two – Death Row Tales Part I

Chapter Three – Death Row Tales Part II

Chapter Four – Karen Johnson Swift

Chapter Five – Henry Greenbaum

Chapter Six – Estelle Laughlin

Chapter Seven – The curious case of Rebekah Gould

Amanda "Mandy" Tusing

"Rain slowly slides down the glass as if the night is crying."

- Patricia Cornwell

It was time for Amanda "Mandy" Tusing to depart.

She was sitting in her fiancé's apartment the night of June 14, 2000, in Jonesboro, Arkansas. Powerful thunderstorms swirled outside. The wind raged, and the rain came in fits and torrents. The man she planned to wed, Matt Ervin, asked her not to go.

The storms continued, and it was 11:30 p.m., too late to drive to the little town of Dell, where her parents lived. On a good day, the drive would take an hour or more along Arkansas 18, a thoroughfare that snakes through a myriad of isolated agricultural towns in the Mississippi Delta. Those towns include Lake City, Black Oak, and Manila.

Hall of Fame musician Johnny Cash grew up in this area, as did international, best-selling author John Grisham.

Mandy was in college and had class in the morning. The young woman's ultimate goal was to be a veterinarian, and she had a part-time job at a vet's office. The 1998 high school graduate had just completed a two-year degree program at Mississippi County Community College, now called Arkansas Northeastern College in Blytheville. She needed to return to her parent's house to ensure she would be in class on time. Amanda made the promise to call when she arrived.

She never made that call.

The 20-year-old, ventured into the rainy night. By all accounts, she was steadily making her way east in the direction of her parent's house when something went horribly wrong.

Two hours after she left, Matt became alarmed. He could not sleep. He called Amanda's dad, Ed Tusing. The father checked in his daughter's room. She was not there. They decided to wait a few more minutes to see if she would finally show up. The storms could have slowed her drive, they reasoned. Minutes later, Matt could wait no longer. He told Ed he was leaving Jonesboro and headed to Dell. Ed and Amanda's twin brother, Andy, departed Dell and headed west.

Mandy had a cell phone, but it was rarely charged. Cell service in those rural areas was often spotty, especially at the dawn of the new century when the technology was still relatively new. Matt reasoned she might have stopped somewhere along the route to let the storms pass, or maybe she had car trouble, although that would have been odd. The 1992 black Pontiac Grand Am she drove was mechanically sound.

Matt was originally from Gosnell, a town not far from Dell. As he drove into the Mississippi Delta, he passed through Bowman, Lake City, and Black Oak. The highway then snakes through the town of Monette. As he drove near the town, he spotted a car parked underneath a streetlight in front of a house. The closer he got the clearer it became.

It was Mandy's car.

He stopped. Moments later, he met Ed and Andy. The car was empty. The keys were still in the ignition. The radio was set to her favorite station, and the volume had been slightly turned down. The windshield wipers were suspended in mid slap, meaning the car was turned off when the rains still pounded. Her wallet was still in the car. A beverage, cold to the touch, sat in the middle console.

The driver's seat was pushed to the front, consistent with Mandy's driving habits. A diploma holder and her blue graduation gown were in the backseat. Her personalized front license plate, emblazoned with her childhood nickname "Sprout" was still fastened to her car.

Fiancé, father, and brother knew something was terribly wrong. They immediately notified police. Bolos were sent out. The 5'1 girl, with blue eyes was last seen wearing a Gap t-shirt, blue jeans, and brown sandals.

An intensive search ensued in the days after Amanda Tusing went missing. The car was transported back to the Craighead County Sheriff's Department for examination. Officers decided to start the car to determine if there had been any mechanical issues.

"That car was sound. It started right up," lead detective and veteran lawman Gary Etter said.

There were no signs of a struggle in the car. Investigators didn't find any footprints near the vehicle. No fingerprints were recovered. Everything in the car appeared to be in place, except for Mandy, he said. She was small in stature, but she was an athlete and aggressive. She would have fought for her life, and would have struggled with anyone attempting to remove her from her own car, Etter said.

"She was feisty ... she'd fight a bear."

The community was flabbergasted by the news of Mandy's disappearance. The people that lived in the house near where her car was found saw and heard nothing. Deshawna Deford was a few grades behind Amanda in high school, but the two had played basketball together. No one could believe she was gone, DeFord said. She was at softball practice when the news broke. Panic ensued.

"There's no way, not her. Things like this don't happen in our town. Everybody loved her," she said.

The agonizing minutes turned to hours and then days. Desolate terrain in eastern Craighead County and adjacent Mississippi County hampered search efforts. Volunteers and officers scoured the region. This part of Arkansas is dotted by flat row crop fields, especially cotton. A series of creeks, rivers, and drainage ditches support the agriculture fields, and the heavy rains made a few places nearly impossible to search.

Blood was discovered on a bridge near the town of Lake City. The harsh weather degraded the blood to the point it was forensically useless, according to investigators.

A couple from the town of Lester was driving on Arkansas 135, near the St. Francis River on June 18, 2000, almost four days after she disappeared. Trent and Fonda Davis were north of Lake City and about 11 miles from where Amanda's car was discovered. As they drove along the Big Bay Ditch, near the Twin Bridges, a pair of blue jeans in the water caught their attention.

To their horror, the couple realized it wasn't a pair of jeans floating in the water. It was a body wearing jeans. Authorities were summoned to the scene. Her body was found about 50 yards east of the bridges. She had been in the water three or four days.

Mandy had no visible signs of body trauma. She was fully clothed and still had a hat on her head that she bought at a store before her disappearance. The woman's driver's license was in the front pocket of her jeans. Her parents told police she had a habit of keeping it there, so this might have been an unimportant detail. Jack McCann, the sheriff at the time, hoped the autopsy would provide them a lead or at least a few clues. The report only compounded their collective frustrations.

The young woman had not been sexually assaulted, and her clothes had never been removed, the medical examiner found. There were no injuries to her genitals or neck. No foreign DNA had been recovered, Etter said. Nothing was found underneath her fingernails. The only wound to her body was a bruise on the back of her head, and it wasn't severe; the medical examiner concluded it could have even occurred after she fell or was placed in the water. Her toxicology report came back normal.

Investigators wanted to know if she suffered any injuries to her wrists. Did her killer restrain her with handcuffs, zip ties, or something else? Forensic examiners concluded she was not restrained.

The cause of death was bizarre, too. The report stated she died from symptoms "consistent with drowning." Little or no water was found in her lungs. It could have been a case of "dry drowning." When a person enters the water, an infusion of liquid through the mouth can cause a muscle spasm and a mucus plug to form. It suffocates the victim. Investigators developed a theory she was suffocated before being dumped in the water, even though she didn't have injuries to her throat. She might have been smothered.

It's possible she was still alive when she entered the water, but she may have been unconscious.

Dry drowning could have occurred if her head was held under water for a length of time. Investigators were certain her body had been placed in the water not far from where it was found, but no meaningful clues were uncovered. During my research into this case, I was told by a person close to the investigation that two, slight symmetrical marks were found on her neck, but the cause was uncertain.

The constant rains had washed potential evidence away. One thing was certain, however. Someone murdered Amanda Tusing. Investigators had no doubt her killer knew the fields, the highways, and the backroads in Craighead County, and he knew them well. He had to be a local. Detectives made multiple trips to the Arkansas State Medical Examiner's Office hoping to find a morsel or nugget that would lead them to her killer. Nothing significant was gleaned.

"We have no doubt it was a homicide," McCann said at the time. "Right now we're up a creek."

As the days and weeks unfolded, Etter became frustrated with the process. A random hair was found on her, and it wasn't DNA tested, initially. Etter wanted to know why. Officials told him the office had a lot of personnel turnover, and it was a simple error. The hair was eventually tested, and it belonged to the dead girl.

Mandy's funeral was held five days after her body had been recovered. DeFord attended the funeral, and she said it was like the "entire town of Dell," and half of Mississippi County attended. Emotions ran deep.

"She is holding God's hand and now resides in heaven. She sees the face of Jesus and sings with the angels. For that alone, I have found some peace, but will continue to feel sorrow till my dying day … The sun will shine with a different light … Mandy's light. Her light will shine on forever," was written in the service program.

She was buried at the Elmwood Cemetery in Blytheville, a town not far from Dell. The Gosnell School District honored Amanda by retiring her number 32 jersey at a ceremony following her death. Matt spoke to the capacity crowd. During her years at Gosnell, she starred as the team's point guard and was an all-conference selection. She also served as a team co-captain during her playing days. The jersey was retired before the first home game that season.

Mandy left behind a grieving family, a shocked community, and perplexed law enforcement officers. She left behind her beloved dog, Baxter, and a fiancé she would never call husband. The two had known each other for five years and had dated for three years.

The road between Dell and Jonesboro was often traveled that summer by the girls who played softball, Deford said. The high school girls played in tournaments and in a league in Jonesboro. They often traveled together for protection. Each time she travelled Arkansas 18, terror filled Deford's mind.

"It was scary. We didn't know what happened to her."

Mandy took the secret of her killer to the grave with her. The unusual case generated national headlines, but remains unsolved. The show "Haunting Evidence" aired an episode profiling her case in 2006. Nothing of real significance was learned. Police spent many years developing leads and clues, but her killer remains a mystery.

A suspect has never been named, but there's significant evidence that points in one direction. There have been many theories as to who killed this young woman, and Etter has investigated all of them.

An explanation of the region's rich history is needed, to give those theories context.

...

This region in Arkansas is historic. It's dominated by agriculture fields. Soybeans, cotton, rice, corn, and others are grown in this relatively flat area. The soil is dark, filled with nutrients from a time when the great Mississippi River flowed further west, and those nutrients were deposited here. Arkansas produces about half the nation's rice, and it's one of the top producers of cotton and soybeans. These fields birth a wide range of makeshift roads, drainage ditches, and levees.

Famous people have come from the region, too. Hall-of-Fame musician Johnny Cash grew up in the tiny town of Dyess in rural Mississippi County. His childhood home has been turned into a museum. I'd written about it several times, but had never visited it before.

In the fall of 2017, the Johnny Cash Festival was underway in Dyess. I had traveled through the area several times during my journalistic career, but it wasn't often. My friend, Mark Randall, and I made the trip to Dyess one Friday afternoon. He was slated to speak at a symposium. Cash, Elvis Presley, Jerry Lee Lewis, and other rock-n-roll immortals used to play at clubs and honky-tonks throughout the south, before fame and fortune swept them away.

After he spoke, we drove out of town. As we drove, he asked me if I'd been to the Cash homestead. I said no. We drove down a long gravel road to reach the house. Row crop fields and ditches surrounded us on each side. Tractors hummed in the fields. The sunshine was bright. When we finally reached the house. Two security guards met us.

A stage was being setup near the house for a planned concert the next day. We asked if we could peek inside the house, and the guards obliged. A tour guide took us through the house. A few minutes in, a guard asked if I could move my car.

I walked outside, and a van appeared in the driveway. Several people, including a woman and a teacup Schnauzer, climbed out of the van. I petted the dog, and said hello to the woman.

"I'm Joanne Cash … I'm Johnny Cash's sister," she said.

Joanne Cash tenderly walked into the family's home place. The tour guide decided to take a break, and let Joanne tell her family story. As she entered the doorway, the first thing she noticed was the piano she played with her mother, Carrie. Often they played while Johnny sang. As she spoke, she suddenly noticed the original floor linoleum, uncovered when the house was restored.

Above her was a quilting rack her mother would pull down to quilt. As she continued to turn, the shadows highlighted her face. Her memories remained vivid. Sunlight that cast through the windows was the only light in the house.

"It seems kind of small now. … Doesn't this bring back the memories," she said.

How the Cash family came to this place in Northeast Arkansas was a common story during a harsh bit of history. Drought, sporadic floods, and the Great Depression decimated family farms in the early 1930s. President Franklin Roosevelt started what was then called a socialistic plan to help many of these farmers in eastern Arkansas.

Ray and Carrie Cash brought their family to the Dyess Colony in 1935, according to historians. During that era, the area was more swamp than usable farm ground. Workers drained the swamp and 500 farm families, including the Cash family, received 40 acres and a mule through a federal government aid program. Cotton was grown. Johnny Cash, along with his brother, Jack, worked the family farm and attended school. Work in the fields was grueling. At night, Johnny and Jack spent a lot of time in their room.

Ray was a strict disciplinarian who worked extremely hard, Joanne said. The children toiled in the cotton fields alongside their parents. Johnny, along with his siblings, was raised in humble circumstances, and the Cash children were taught to work for what they earned, she said. The family was at the mercy of cotton prices.

When Joanne walked back into the room in which Johnny slept, she smiled. Their brother, Tommy, and Johnny shared the same bed for several years. He joked about it often, she said.

"Tommy likes to tell people that he's the only man who has ever slept with Johnny Cash," she said to a chorus of laughter from those now following her through the house.

When the tour ended, we left the house down the same unforgiving gravel road.

Another legend spent his childhood here, and his family roots are very near the spot where Mandy was abducted.

Best-selling author John Grisham was born and lived part of his childhood in Northeast Arkansas. Grisham was born Feb. 8, 1955, in Jonesboro. His father was a construction worker and his mother was a homemaker. The family was tight knit.

The future author spent many hours on his family's farm. His vivid descriptions of rural life in the South were derived from these childhood experiences. His novel, "A Painted House," is based on his experiences in the cotton fields near Black Oak. The actual "Painted House," the set used in the movie of the same name is located in Lepanto. It's one of the few Grisham books outside the legal thriller genre. It's not as well known as some of his other books such as "The Firm" or "A Time to Kill," but it gives a portrayal of the cultural landscape.

Part of Grisham's family hails from Black Oak, the last town Mandy passed through. Black Oak is an insignificant dot on a map to motorists. Each fall, seas of white cotton inundate the fields in and around the town. Only a few hundred people still live here. People in this town are quiet and keep to themselves. Church is on Sundays and Wednesdays. Kids play baseball and softball in the spring and summer. In the winter, they play basketball.

It was in this quintessential piece of Americana that death knocked on Mandy's car door.

Theories

Amanda Tusing was a case that as an investigative journalist I had avoided for many years. I'd written about nearly every major murder case in the region during the last 15 years, but for some reason this story eluded me. I remember when it happened, and the fear it inspired. The world was much different in 2000.

The internet was only six years old, and cell phone use was sporadic. Social media hadn't been invented. The economy was strong and we had just finished the Bill Clinton impeachment scandal. I've often heard Mr. Clinton say this part of the state saved his political career after he lost his bid for a second term as Arkansas's governor in 1980, but regained the office a few years later after spending a lot of time reconnecting with voters in Northeast Arkansas. The controversial Bush vs. Gore presidential election loomed, and the society changing attacks on Sept. 11, 2001, were more than a year away.

A listlessness seemed to have crept into society. It was shattered in this part of the country by the events in the early morning hours of June 15, 2000. After her body had been retrieved, the investigation was turned over to Etter.

Etter has spent nearly 48 years working in law enforcement. He was hired in 1971 as a patrol officer in Jonesboro, and when he retired, he took a new job with the Craighead County Sheriff's Department in 1997. Throughout his career, he has investigated many criminal cases, but one stands above the rest, the murder of Mandy Tusing.

When I decided to write about this case, I researched it for several weeks. I arranged to talk to several officers involved, but the fulcrum was Etter. He learned I was trying to track down Mandy's family, so he did what any good detective would do. He tracked me down.

Every few weeks he talks with Susan Tusing, the girl's mother. During his 18-year involvement in the case, he's interviewed about 300 people, and chased dozens of leads. I interviewed him in early 2018.

"It's still an active case. I'm still interviewing people. This case is still open," he told me.

The bizarre details such as the key in the ignition, her wallet still in the car, the radio station, the wiper blades, and her license in her front pocket, and the lack of a struggle in the car indicates she left willingly or was scared to the point of not resisting, Etter said.

Her hat was still on her head, the lack of any evidence of a sexual assault, and the fact she still had her engagement ring on her finger when her body was found, meant a couple of possibilities could be ruled out.

The first theory squashed was that Mandy was a victim of a robbery gone wrong. Her ring was still on her finger and her wallet was in the car. No thief would have missed those two things.

A second, more plausible theory that gained traction was she was the victim of a transient serial killer. Many in the national media speculated how this case was similar to abduction cases in states such as Ohio, Florida, Tennessee, and others. Etter was able to dismiss this possibility.

Where her body was discovered is extremely rural. To get the body into that waterway would have been difficult, and the main entry point is mostly known only to locals.

Someone without intimate knowledge of the region would have never found that spot, he said.

"It was someone who knew the area," he said. "It wasn't a drifter. Whoever did this knew the area."

A natural suspect in the case was her fiancée, Matt Ervin. In cases like these, investigators say it's not uncommon for a husband or boyfriend to kill a spouse or girlfriend in a rage-fueled fit. Police interrogated Ervin, but his story remained consistent. He was very cooperative with detectives and agreed to multiple polygraph exams, which he easily passed. One witness claimed to have seen Mandy at a convenience store that night, but surveillance cameras couldn't confirm if she was in there. The beverage in her car may have come from Ervin's apartment, but he couldn't remember if she grabbed one or not.

His apartment was searched, but no evidence was found.

The two had a minor quarrel about him possibly attending college in Mississippi, but it wasn't serious, Etter said. The couple planned to wed in June 2001. Mandy's family stood by him and steadfastly said he had nothing to do with her murder. He spoke at the ceremony at the Gosnell High School to retire her jersey.

Etter and another officer were in Little Rock long after the murder, and decided to stop in and visit Ervin. He had moved to sell insurance. He welcomed the officers into his office. He offered to take yet another polygraph, and it was arranged. The examiner said he easily passed.

"Anything we asked him to do, he did it," Etter said. "He was very cooperative. He didn't have anything to do with Mandy's murder."

The research I'd done led me to the same conclusion, even before I spoke to the detective. Many have speculated on social media sites that he might be involved in some manner, but I don't think so.

One thing murderers don't typically do is alert the police and family members about a missing or murdered person. No one would have looked for her that night if he hadn't been worried and called her parents. Matt may have passed the actual killer on the road when he was searching for his girlfriend, a chilling thought.

This theory was easily eliminated.

Rumors started from the beginning the killing was related to drug activity. Etter and other investigators have conducted countless interviews with people involved in drugs throughout the region. Many claimed to have insider knowledge about her death.

One person claimed Mandy was at a party prior to her disappearance, and she was involved in drug activity. This person said she owed money, and when she didn't pay her debt, she was killed. A Manila woman claimed she had knowledge of the murder, and was interviewed in 2003, but nothing useful was gleaned. Etter chased down these leads for years. This theory was easily disproved.

"That was not Mandy … she wasn't involved in anything like that," he said.

Speculation was rampant that illegal drug activity was involved, but that Mandy's death was the result of mistaken identity.

Drugs such as methamphetamine, marijuana, heroin, cocaine, and others are trafficked at a high rate in eastern Arkansas. The reason is simple. It's close to key highway arteries that connect the rest of the country and North America. U.S. 55 runs from Canada to Mexico. Chicago, St. Louis, Memphis, and New Orleans sit along its path. So does Blytheville. Drugs from other countries and big cities are often moved on this route and through Blytheville. Not far from Blytheville, U.S. 40, which connects the east and west coasts, intersects in the town of West Memphis.

For years, rumors persisted a drug gang roamed the highway that night in search of a black Pontiac Grand Am, and that Mandy was mistakenly stopped by the gang. This too, proved untrue. Those killed by drug gangs are not simply smothered or drowned. If this were the case, Mandy likely would have been shot or stabbed. This theory made no sense to me.

I've been told during the course of numerous drug investigations, undercover agents have broached Mandy's name. Druggies may claim to have information about this case when talking to police, but in their dark underworld no significant information surfaced. Undercover agents asked questions about the death, but no one seemed to have a clue. I've covered drug-related cases for many years and have written about murders connected to those cases. At some point, one of those druggies would have talked.

A deafening silence met agents when questions about Mandy's death were asked.

The peculiar details in the case led investigators down one path, a haunting one. The evidence seemed to point towards Mandy stopping at the behest of a trusted figure – a police officer. It could have been someone impersonating a police officer, like the "blue-light" rapist. Etter is certain it was a police officer or someone impersonating one that stopped Mandy.

"When she was stopped she saw either blue or red lights behind her. I'm sure of that."

There was a blue-light rapist in Arkansas just a couple of years before Mandy's death.

Shannon Woods, 17, drove Arkansas 38 in Lonoke County on July 11, 1997. She was on her way home. Suddenly, blue lights lit the darkness in her rear-view mirror. She slowed, and pulled to the side of the road. The girl grabbed her license and expected a speeding ticket. She expected a cop to tap on her window.

Instead, she was met by a man wearing a ski mask and totting a gun. The man, 32-year-old Robert Todd Burmingham of St. Francis County, ordered Woods into his car. They drove 80 miles near the town of Brinkley. Woods was taken to a house where she was blindfolded. Burmingham spent hours raping the teen.

He released her face down in a busy intersection following the attack. Woods was able to provide police key clues that led to the man's arrest. He was linked to four rapes initiated by his blue lights. The story made national headlines.

Reports of others attempting to stop women using blue lights have appeared periodically around Arkansas and across the country. However, there was no other verified report of a blue light rapist impersonator trolling the area where Mandy was abducted, Etter said. No other woman was stopped or harmed by someone flashing a blue light and pretending to be a cop. Investigators chased these leads, too. The trail went cold. There's no evidence a person was impersonating a police officer the night Mandy went missing.

It leads to the only logical conclusion one can surmise from the evidence released in this case. Mandy was abducted and killed by a legitimate law officer. The evidence so strongly pointed in that direction, the police polygraphed and interviewed law officers who worked or lived in eastern Craighead County and in Mississippi County. When the dust settled and the interviews were complete, one officer became the primary suspect, even if he wasn't officially named as one.

I've dealt with many law officers through the years, and I have a high level of respect for the men and women that spend their lives protecting our rights and freedoms. In every profession, there can be a rogue. Police officers often work without any supervision and alone. They patrol lonely stretches of road at night, and the opportunities to engage in deviant behaviors are abundant. In addition, there were more opportunities to engage in this type of behavior before the age of the internet and cell phones.

I was at the gym one day discussing my theory about this case with a friend. I told him there are several under-reported crimes, and one of them is sexual misconduct between officers and female motorists. A study released by Bowling Green University analyzed the phenomenon.

Cases of sex-related misconduct and crime have been described as hidden offenses that are likely to go unreported and, hence, difficult to document and study, the study states.

Victims may not report instances of police sexual misconduct to authorities because they feel humiliated or they may fear retaliation. Victims may also encounter barriers to filing a complaint since that process can be unnecessarily difficult and/or intimidating. Researchers are also hard-pressed for data on cases that do get officially reported because of the reluctance of officers and organizations to expose cases of sex related police misconduct to outside scrutiny.

Obstacles in acquiring official data detailing the phenomenon are numerous. It often requires a court order and it can be difficult to get one. American police departments typically do not collect and distribute data on coercive police practices.

Data had to be compiled by using a range of alternative methodologies including surveys, interviews, published federal court opinions, and limited news searches. The existing line of research has clearly advanced knowledge over the course of three decades; but much of what is known about sex-related police misconduct derives from research that is either purely qualitative or based on a comparatively small sample of cases, according to the study.

In other words, when this crime occurs, victims rarely report it, and when they do, agencies are not keen to publicize it.

As the conversation with my friend deepened, I told him a classic scenario. Imagine a late night on a sparsely traveled road. Suddenly, headlights appear in the darkness. A young woman is on her way home from frolicking with her friends. A police officer stops her. Maybe she's been drinking, or maybe not. He checks her license and then asks her to step out of her vehicle. They go back to his car. In order to avoid a ticket, she is asked to perform a sex act. The officer threatens retaliation if she doesn't comply.

In the heat of the moment, she agrees. How many times has this happened? Who would tell after the fact? How could she prove it days, weeks, or even months later?

My friend vehemently disagreed. He didn't think police officers could or would do something so despicable. I agreed most would not, and in an age where everyone has a phone and police have cameras in their cars and on their bodies, it would be much more difficult. However, in 2000, and the decades before that, it wasn't the case. Mandy had a cell phone, but it was often not charged, and service was scant.

A veteran police officer, one with knowledge of the area and familiar with the types of vehicles and driving habits of female drivers, would easily be able to locate women. She frequented the highway, and the officer may have known her driving habits and times.

My friend continued to believe those women would expose a rogue cop committing these acts. I told him there are many victims in society that chose to keep their terrible secrets. Our culture has changed in recent years, but those changes are recent I reminded him.

One key clue in Mandy's case, according to Etter was the location where she was found. Her car was located on the highway near Monette. Her body was found 11 miles away, north of Lake City. The person that took Mandy had precise knowledge of the roadways.

The killer was likely a local police officer, in my estimation.

A Craighead County deputy from Black Oak lived a few miles from where Mandy's car was found. He was well known in his community and was known to rove the highways at night in his patrol car.

The deputy was Johnny Williams.

Williams was a longtime officer. He lived and breathed police work, from what I'm told. Even on his days off, he would come to the sheriff's office.

An unnamed man told investigators he saw Mandy's car stopped by a police officer that night. The man couldn't remember the exact time or place, but said he would be able to recognize the car if he saw it. Investigators showed him several different types of police patrol cars common to the area, including the Arkansas State Police and others. He didn't recognize any of them. The last car he was shown was a Craighead County patrol car and he instantly identified the distinctive markings.

Social media sites are filled with volumes of inaccurate reports and accusations. Sites like this can provide investigators a smidgen of value, however. In this case, there is an avalanche of posts detailing Williams' alleged behavior. One woman claimed he would stop her constantly and follow her home.

"Johnny Williams has always been a pervert when young girls come into play. He followed me around. At the time of the murder, I worked in Jonesboro from 2 p.m. to 10 p.m. He would follow me all the way to my home at times. I've heard all along he's the one who did this."

Another woman said he stalked her friend's home multiple times.

"This man followed one of my girlfriends more times than once. He even followed her to her house and parked by her driveway on many occasions. She called me one night to ask me to find the city cop ... she was scared out of her wits!" one person wrote.

The accounts on social media match what was being told to young female drivers that frequented the highway. What that could mean is there is some level of accuracy in those posts.

Williams became a suspect early in the investigation. He was interviewed and asked about the case more than once. Other law officers were interrogated and eliminated as suspects. He was at the top of the list and nothing learned during the interviews with law officers changed the theory that it could be Johnny Williams, according to detectives.

There are a few in the Arkansas State Police who think he was involved in the murder of another woman in Poinsett County.

Barbara Bryan, 30, a mother of two was found shot to death along Arkansas 181, a highway in rural Mississippi County near the town of Victoria, on Dec. 12, 1980. She was shot twice at close range with a shotgun, according to the State Medical Examiner. Her car was found locked five miles away.

Bryan's purse and other personal items were not taken. Robbery was ruled out. Whoever lured Bryan out of her car was someone she trusted. The Lepanto native was reportedly dating Williams at the time. A police officer was interviewed in the case, but investigators never officially named Williams as a suspect. I spoke to a source close to this investigation who spoke to me on the condition of anonymity. Williams was the primary suspect, and hours after her body was found, detectives went to Williams' home. He was known to be "sloppy" with his equipment in police circles. When they examined his shotgun, it was "clean as a whistle." Someone spent hours cleaning that weapon before it was examined, my source told me.

Investigators couldn't establish a motive. Leads were followed, and multiple interviews were conducted, but Bryan's killer was never brought to justice.

A former Arkansas State Police officer told me there was no doubt in the law enforcement community at that time that Williams murdered Bryan. There wasn't enough evidence to link him to the crime, however. Ironically, for me, the prosecutor overseeing the case was David Burnett. He would later become a judge and preside over the West Memphis Three case, the subject of my first book, "Witches in West Memphis … and another false confession."

I attempted to contact her family for this story, but was unable to track them down. I told friends if they wanted to talk I would be glad to listen, but I understand if they chose not to. I'm not sure what the family theory is about this case.

During my research into the Bryan case, I sent a social media message out asking for information. I received a flood of responses, mostly from women, that detailed Williams's behavior. One woman sent me this message:

"She (Bryan) was dating Johnny Williams at the time. They couldn't prove that he did it, so they fired him from Poinsett County Sheriff's Department. He's also the one I believe killed Mandy. Johnny followed my sister-in-law from Jonesboro to Lake City after Mandy's murder. Her son was with her as was my brother (in a separate car). Her son had to pee so they went down the levee. Johnny followed so my brother stopped. Johnny pulled up beside them and says, "Hey girl what are you doing out here all alone?" My brother spoke up and Johnny changed his tune and claimed to just be checking on them. My niece's car broke down on Arkansas 18 just outside of Black Oak, and at the time, there was a pay phone at Black Oak Fire Department. While her and her friend were using the phone, Johnny pulled up and tried to get them to go with him. They refused, and he got demanding about it so they ran to the house next door which happens to be my sister's house. Johnny then took off."

I don't know if any of these stories are true, but I've read and received too many messages to think there isn't some truth in these stories. The onslaught of messages was never ending. Coupled with the conversations I've had with law officers about Williams, there is no doubt he harassed female motorists.

As other leads and suspects were eliminated in Mandy's murder, the focus turned to Williams. He was interrogated. I'm told that during one interview he was asked directly if he killed the girl. Williams paused, looked up, and acted as if he would affirm the statement. He then backtracked and said he had no connection to the murder.

Many in the community believed Williams was involved in the murders, and suspected the Craighead County Sheriff's Department was protecting one of their own. I don't think that was the case. Naming him as a suspect to the public would have brought on a litany of problems.

There was no forensic or physical evidence that tied him to the crime. I'm not privy to any alibi he may have given investigators, but I'm sure they confirmed it. The crime lacked evidence. Charging him without a confession would have been difficult in my estimation. I know investigators grilled him several times. However, he knew just as they did, without a confession, it would be nearly impossible to tie the murder to him.

The years went by and no new information in the case surfaced. Williams got cancer and in 2009 was near death. Investigators attempted to coax a deathbed confession from him, but were unsuccessful. Williams's health rebounded, but several months later he died from congestive heart failure, I'm told. He was 61.

I cannot imagine the pain Mandy's family goes through each day. She has two brothers, one a twin, and two parents who obviously loved her very much. I tried to reach out to them while writing this story, but they opted not to talk. I completely understand. In the past, I've always pushed hard to talk with family members for stories like this.

This time I decided to let it go. My goal in this endeavor is to get this crime solved. I don't know if Williams killed her. The facts in the case leave little doubt it was a law officer. None of the other scenarios makes sense. The person that took Mandy's life did so for only one reason.

She could identify him. She would have told.

Is it possible it was a police impersonator? Yes, but it would be a stretch. There were no reports of a person using blue lights to stop women in that part of Arkansas before, during, or after her murder. Investigators, including former Sheriff Jack McCann, have said that from day one it was a local with intimate knowledge of the roadways and rural areas.

There is also the question of motive. The blue light rapist stopped women to rape them. Anyone using a blue light would have a motive in stopping those women. She was not raped or tortured.

Why would an impersonator go through this much trouble just to drive her out to a remote spot and kill her? Why didn't this person act again?

I think anyone impersonating a cop to stop women at night would have to be motivated by strong sexual or control desires that would not have been satisfied by simply taking her to a waterway and holding her head underwater. Doesn't make sense to me.

It is possible, however, Mandy might have been the first time this impersonator had tried to copycat the previous blue light rapist's tactics, and it went wrong when she wouldn't submit. After this failure, maybe the would-be rapist gave up. I think an impersonator would have still had sex with her before killing her. An officer would know committing that act would be violent and leave evidence, such as hairs and DNA.

This is how I think Mandy's last hours unfolded. She left her boyfriend's house at 11:30 p.m., June 14, 2000. He told her to call when she reached home. Mandy grabbed a drink at his house or stopped to grab one on the way home. She drove Arkansas 18 in the wind and rain.

The rains became so intense she may have pulled over on the side of the road outside of Monette. Blue and red lights flashed and she was compelled to stop. Her seat was pushed all the way forward, her wallet was sitting in the passenger seat. The radio blared songs from her favorite station.

An officer approached. She turned down the radio and rolled down her window.

"License and registration," he likely said.

He gave her some reason as to why he stopped her. He tells her he needs to check her driver's license. She smiles and obliges the officer. He takes her license and returns to his patrol car. I'm sure a motorist passed and saw the stopped vehicles. How common is it to see blue lights and a car stopped on the side of the road at night? Others that lived in nearby houses reported seeing blue lights in the vicinity that night, and one even told police it was curious because the storms still raged. Why would a police officer stop someone in a storm like this?

The officer returns. It's still raining. He tells Mandy he needs to speak with her in his police cruiser. It's nothing to worry about, but he needs to chat with her for a second. The unsuspecting girl exits her car. She leaves the car keys in the ignition. She will return, momentarily. Mandy places her driver's license in her front pocket as she enters the dark, rainy night. Once in the car, the officer drives away.

He knows the back roads and out-of-the-way places in eastern Craighead County well. I do not know what she thought or knew at this point. Maybe he told her a ruse about rushing to another call, and there was no time to let her out of the car. He took her to a desolate spot down a series of gravel roads outside of Lake City, near where her body was eventually found.

His intentions are now obvious. He wants her to commit a sexual act with him. He miscalculated. Mandy was a fiercely independent woman, loyal to the man she planned to marry. She would not betray him or herself. This officer had done this with other women, and it had worked.

Not tonight.

Mandy prepared to fight. The officer knew in that moment his way of life was about to end. He was wearing his uniform. His car could be identified. Mandy saw his face and name badge. There was no turning back. His career as a police officer, something he cherished, was about to end.

Unless, he got rid of the witness.

Mandy would have fought, but she might not have in one instance. Etter said if she was scared, she might not fight back. There was only one, minor bruise to the back of her head, and two slight marks on her neck.

The officer brandished his firearm and ordered her out of the car. Terrified, she exits the vehicle. He walks her to the water's edge. At this moment, he pushes her in. He holds her head underwater. A mucus plug forms and the muscles inside her neck spasm. A minute or two later the aspiring veterinarian, the girl who loved animals, her fiancé, her brothers, and her mom and dad, floated lifeless in the water. The action was so swift, so sudden; he didn't even knock the hat from her head.

Once he's sure she is dead, he exits the scene. Not long after this, her boyfriend, dad, and twin brother come upon the car. There's no footprints in or around the car. There is no evidence of a struggle. Everything was in its place in that perfectly working car except for one thing – Mandy.

The two marks on her neck are intriguing. It's possible she might have been subdued with a stun gun, fell unconscious in the police car, and then her killer dumped her body from one of the bridges near where her body was found. This theory is interesting, but more evidence would have to surface to prove it.

For years, her mother, Susan Tusing, has publicly stated she thinks a police officer or an impersonator killed her daughter. It wasn't an impersonator. Someone impersonating an officer would have raped or tortured her. The true killer had to murder Mandy because she could and would have identified him, plain and simple. I trust a mother's instincts in this regard.

I think a police officer killed Mandy Tusing.

Was it Williams? I don't know. Reportedly, there was a state trooper patrolling the area that night, as well. I don't know if that report has ever been fully vetted by the police, but it's another possibility.

Williams' transgressions are well known in law enforcement circles, and his antics towards female motorists have been talked about and documented in the communities he worked in for many years. He lived a few miles from where the abduction took place, and was known to patrol the highways off-duty.

He was a cop's cop. His life was wrapped in law enforcement. He would have lost it all if she would have reported his behavior. The contents and positioning of her car suggest she was stopped by a police officer.

I don't think the Craighead County Sheriff's Department is involved in a cover-up in this case, as some have speculated. Without a confession, it would be an extremely hard case to make in court despite the powerful circumstantial evidence.

I've thought a lot about Mandy Tusing through the years. People in this part of the world still talk about her case to this day. I still hold out hope that the pieces to solve this puzzle will someday be discovered. If Williams killed her, maybe he confessed his deed to another person. Probably not. Loose lips, not fancy detective work, solve most crimes. He knew that. If he's the perpetrator, he probably took his secret to the grave.

The known evidence in the case points in his direction, but to be fair things could change with new evidence. In 2013, I covered the murder of another Gosnell girl, 11-year-old

Jessica Williams. She was in her yard playing with her puppy, Ryback, on Aug. 27, 2013, when she vanished. Her father, Eric, began searching the adjacent gravel roads in rural Mississippi County near Gosnell. Neighbors joined the effort.

One neighbor, Freddie Sharp III, found the girl's bike on the side of the road. The afternoon soon turned to twilight and then darkness. In the blackness, the search intensified with no results. Two girls found Ryback walking down a road, 11 miles away the next morning.

Searchers took the dog back to the spot where he was found. The dog instinctively took them to a drainage ditch where Jessica's body had been discarded. Police began a homicide investigation.

Soon after a neighbor, 17-year-old Christopher Sowell, confessed. He rode the school bus with Jessica, and even helped her dad search for her. Now, he was a murderer, according to his own words. A gag order was placed on the case by a judge.

Sowell was held in the Mississippi County Jail awaiting his trial. Prosecutors and police remained tight-lipped, but they believed they had the right person. His statement to police was damning.

"Sowell stated upon Jessica's arrival he became angry with her," Mississippi County Sheriff's Department Sgt. Brice Hicks stated in a probable cause affidavit. "Sowell stated he … grabbed Jessica by the throat and choked her until she became 'wide-eyed.' He then pushed her over the side of the bridge into the water and walked away."

Questions remained, however. Sowell didn't have a vehicle and was searching for Jessica with her father almost as soon as the girl went missing. The gag order prevented anyone from talking. Several months came and went.

Then one piece of evidence completely changed the case.

A single sperm cell was recovered from the girl's body. It was DNA tested, and it didn't match Sowell. It matched Sharp, the person who found her bike on the side of the road. He knew where it was because that's where he abducted her. Had that one sperm cell not been found, Sowell would be in prison for the rest of his life, or he would be on Arkansas' Death Row. Sharp would be roaming the streets a free man.

One piece of evidence could appear and change the trajectory of this entire case, but I doubt it. The passage of time and the lack of any physical evidence from the original investigation mean there's little chance.

To this day, I still catch people talking about Amanda Tusing. It's almost like an urban legend, the tale of a beloved college-aged girl that vanished without a trace in the middle of the night. The fear it inspired still resonates with some to this day.

Deford lived through the fear of driving Arkansas 18. It was common knowledge a police officer or someone impersonating one roamed. During her life, Deford has been stopped several times.

"I get scared every time … when I see a car following too close … it bothers me," she said. "When I see those blue lights in the mirror I get a lot of anxiety. It makes me nervous."

Etter was slated to retire in August 2018, and I'm told he's no longer with the Craighead County Sheriff's Department as of this writing. I'm not sure what detective will take up the curious case of what happened to Amanda Tusing. Her mother was hopeful the case would be solved before he retired Etter once told me.

"She said I can't retire until I solve Mandy's case. This thing is still a mystery to me … I feel like I know Mandy. I know just about everything about her," he said.

Death Row Tales Part I

"Death comes to us all; we can only choose how to face it when it comes."

- Robert Jordan

A man slated to die for a crime he did not commit was leery to return to the state that tried to kill him. He was released from prison after 18 years of wrongful incarceration in 2011, and he returned almost six years later to protest a series of planned executions, including men he personally knew.

It was a wretchedly hot day when I arrived on the capitol grounds in Little Rock in early April 2017. The state of Arkansas had decided to execute eight Death Row inmates during the last two weeks of that month, because the state's supply of drugs used in executions was set to expire. It would be the most executions undertaken by a state in half a century. This decision roused fury from activists around the country. I was a journalist working for Talk Business & Politics, one of the largest media companies in the state. I was there to cover an anti-execution rally.

A thousand or more gathered at the capitol steps. Media members stood near the speaker's podium. The decision to kill so many prisoners so quickly – Arkansas had not executed a prisoner since 2005 – garnered national attention. As I stood in the baking sun, something near the steps caught my eye. Actor Johnny Depp, former Arkansas Death Row inmate Damien Echols, his wife Lorri, and a couple of bodyguards huddled nearby.

Unbelievably, nobody noticed them.

This wasn't my first encounter with Echols. I'd interviewed him while he sat on Death Row in 2010 after he wrote me a letter. He and his cohorts, Jason Baldwin and Jessie Misskelley Jr., were released from prison Aug. 19, 2011, after the trio agreed to Alford pleas, a legal agreement similar to a no contest plea. They spent 18 years in prison for the deaths of three 8-year-old boys in West Memphis on May 5, 1993. The plea allowed them to be immediately released from state custody.

Stevie Branch, Christopher Byers, and Michael Moore were riding bikes in their West Memphis neighborhood when they vanished around sunset. Prosecutors claim the boys entered a patch of woods near their homes dubbed "Robin Hood Hills," by locals. The three boys were bludgeoned during an attack prosecutors say was inspired by Satanism or a belief in the occult.

The boys were beaten, tortured, and sexually assaulted during the attack, prosecutors theorized. Their clothes were removed, and their hands and feet were bound ankle to wrist. Baldwin emasculated Byers with a knife. The boys' bodies were then tossed into a drainage ditch and drowned.

One month later, the three teens from the nearby town of Marion were charged with the murders, after Misskelley confessed to the crime and implicated the others. The confession contained inaccuracies including the time and place of the murders, the manner in which they were performed, and he told police two of the boys were sexually assaulted when autopsy results showed no sexual assault took place.

Despite the inaccuracies and no physical or forensic evidence tying the teens to the crimes, two juries found them guilty. Echols was sentenced to death while the other two received life terms.

The three teens dubbed "The West Memphis Three" languished in obscurity until the 1996 documentary "Paradise Lost: The Child Murders at Robin Hood Hills" was released by HBO. Doubts surfaced whether the teens committed the crimes. The documentary saved Echols' life, he said. The circumstantial case and the lack of evidence raised doubts among supporters, a group that included Depp, Pearl Jam lead man Eddie Vedder, Dixie Chicks lead singer Natalie Maines, and the director, Sir Peter Jackson. Millions of dollars were raised in an attempt to free the men.

By 2011, Arkansas officials were under pressure to resolve the flawed case. A new trial was about to be ordered. New DNA evidence had been discovered implicating Stevie Branch's stepfather, Terry Hobbs. A hair found in the ligatures that bound Michael Moore was a virtual genetic match for him, and a hair found on a tree stump next to where the bodies were dumped was a genetic match for his alibi witness at the time of the murders, David Jacoby. Hobbs and Jacoby have denied involvement in the murders.

One witness who testified during Misskelley's trial, Victoria Hutcheson, signed a sworn affidavit saying she lied at the trial. During an interview with me in 2009, she admitted she was under pressure from police to provide evidence and was facing a credit card fraud charge. Her son, Aaron was friends with the victims, and he claimed, for a time, to have witnessed the murders, but his statements proved false. She told jurors she attended a "witches gathering" or esbat with Echols and Misskelley. It was a lie. Testimony from another witness who claimed to have heard Echols and Baldwin talking about the murders at a softball game would have likely been disproved during a new trial, prosecutors admitted.

I eyed Echols and Depp and grabbed my notepad sitting on the ground. I stealthily walked towards them. No other reporters moved. As I got closer, it was clear Echols looked nervous. As I approached, a bodyguard started to step in front of me, but Lorri recognized me. We hugged. I turned to Damien. The last time I saw him was the day he was released from prison.

"I haven't seen you in a while … you don't make it back to Arkansas much," I said to him.

"Do you blame me?" he said with a rhetorical smile. At that moment, the media herd scrambled towards us. I stood with Damien and Depp. Cameras flashed. Reporters seemed ready to pounce, but no one would ask a question. I turned to Damien and began the interview. I asked him how it felt to be back in Arkansas.

"I'm back here ... this is where they tried to kill me," Echols said. "They (the state) can make mistakes ... look at me." He later added, "I would have been one of those eight."

He knew many of the men slated for death, including one named Don Davis. He claimed Davis saved his life while the two lived on Death Row. How Davis arrived on Death Row is unthinkable.

...

Don Davis roamed a Rogers-area neighborhood Oct. 12, 1990, in northwest Arkansas looking to rob homes. In one home, he stole a number of items including a television, microwave, an arsenal of guns, and other items. He stacked his stolen goods in his car. He needed a place to hide.

He parked his car in a garage in one of the houses. The homeowners were gone.

At 10 p.m., businessman Richard Daniel returned to his home in the same neighborhood. He was immediately alarmed when he walked in the door and found a Kool cigarette butt in a bowl of rice in the kitchen. Neither he, nor his wife, 62-year-old Jane Daniel smoked. He searched the house. He found her dead in a storeroom. She'd been shot in the head execution style.

The same day Jane Daniel was murdered, Davis returned to his apartment and his roommates told authorities he was acting nervous. He often brought stolen goods to the apartment, but this day he acted different. He told them someone had been injured during one of his burglaries. The items in his possession at the time matched ones stolen from the houses. Eventually, he confessed to his companions.

"I don't know why I shot her, she was cooperating," he reportedly said to friends.

Davis was arrested, convicted, and sentenced to death.

Echols became acquainted with Don Davis, who is no relation to his wife, Lorri Davis-Echols, after he arrived on the Death Row unit in 1994. In prison, you don't really make friends, but you form bonds with people who will "have your back," Echols told me. Davis was one of his confidants.

Davis, who suffers from a low IQ according to his defense attorneys, has said more than once he regrets killing Daniel and doesn't know why he pulled the trigger. The murder haunted Davis in his prison cell late at night, Echols said. The images of the innocent woman tormented him, and he often cried when talking about what he did.

"It's like watching somebody's soul broken wide open," he said.

Echols spent a stint in solitary confinement. He claims the guards wouldn't feed him, and Davis found ways to sneak him morsels of food. It was this act of kindness that compelled Echols and Depp to rally against the executions. A few months later, Echols told me he suffers from severe bouts of depression and post-traumatic stress disorder, PTSD. He claims both are a result of his treatment in prison.

Before I left him, his wife, and Depp to the media vultures, I asked Depp for one personal act. I took a picture of him with Lorri to send to my daughter. She was supposed to make the trip with me, but opted to stay in bed. I sent it to her, and she could not believe it. He smiled and shook my hand.

As I walked away, I was sure this would be the last story I would write about the executions. Arkansas's Death Row unit is on the Arkansas Department of Correction campus outside of the town of Grady, in a remote stretch in southern Arkansas. It was four hours from the town I lived in at the time, and we had another reporter slated to cover it. The likelihood of the executions occurring wasn't high, but just before they started, I decided I might cover one or more of them for the experience of doing it.

Arkansas prepared to execute eight inmates before its lethal drug cocktail expired on May 1. It seemed like lunacy at the time to many outside the state, but inevitably, several of the scheduled executions were stayed by court orders. One that seemed likely to move forward was inmate Ledell Lee's.

Lee's dubious place in history was set into motion by a series of rapes and murders, culminating with one of the most pointless acts of violence I have ever covered as a journalist.

...

Debra Reese was curling her hair mid-morning at her home on Cherry Street in Jacksonville, Ark., on Feb. 9, 1993, when there was a knock at the door. A stranger wanted to borrow some tools. Reese, 26, only had a tire tool her husband left to protect her when he was out of town driving a truck. She told the man she did not have any tools.

She called her mother who lived only five houses away. Reese was scared. She told her mother, Katherine Williams, she didn't trust the guy. Reese promised her mother she would come to her house once she was done curling her hair.

Reese never talked to her mother again.

The stranger, who turned out to be Lee, returned and broke into Reese's home moments later. A neighbor, Andy Gomez, watched Lee enter the home, and leave about 20 minutes afterwards. In the interim, Lee took the tire iron and struck Reese 36 times. He stole $300 from her purse. He had just been released from jail on a burglary charge.

Gomez was suspicious and tailed Lee when he left the Reese house. The murderer used the stolen money to pay several debts that afternoon, including one owed to a nearby Rent-A-Center. Lee was arrested and charged with capital murder. He was convicted and sentenced to death.

Lee had been previously convicted on two separate rape charges, and may have been involved in the murder of a Jacksonville prostitute whose body was dumped in a shed next to railroad tracks. He is also the prime suspect in the abduction, rape, and murder of 22-year-old Christine Lewis in November 1989 in Jacksonville. Lewis was in her home when Lee abducted her. Lewis's 3-year-old child watched as the abduction took place. Her body was found days later in the closet of an abandoned house. She had been raped and strangled.

DNA linked Lee to the rapes and murders. Prosecutors declined to pursue murder charges in the Lewis case after the Arkansas Supreme Court affirmed his death sentence in the Reese case. He was slated to die April 20, 2017.

The day of Lee's execution, I drove south to the Arkansas Department of Correction campus at Varner. It turned out my bosses thought we might need two reporters at the executions, so my trip had a dual purpose.

I made the trek south. The sun was blinding and the air muggy; my body hummed with anticipation. I hate to admit it, but moments like this in a journalist's career are memorable.

Don Davis had been spared by the courts days earlier. His brush with death was close. A few days before Lee's scheduled execution, Davis was slated to die by lethal injection. As his case meandered through the courts that afternoon, he prepared to die. Davis ate one last meal of fried chicken, mashed potatoes, great northern beans, and strawberry cake. He drank fruit punch.

Witnesses waited in the Death Chamber while the U.S. Supreme Court mulled a stay of execution for Davis handed down by the Arkansas Supreme Court earlier in the day. At 11:50 p.m., a full 10 minutes before his death warrant was set to expire, the U.S. Supreme Court decided not to lift the stay, and Davis was spared. Months later, he tried to fire his legal team and drop his life saving appeal, but the courts would not allow him to do so. Apparently, he wants his Death Row tenure to end.

I raced to the Death Row unit. As I arrived on the campus just outside of the town of Grady, I was met by a long row of vehicles. Many were journalists from newspapers, television, online, and others. A few were local, but many were from around the country and the world.

I had a jacket and dress shirt in my car, but had chosen to wear a cutoff gym shirt during the drive. It caused a little suspicion among the guards manning the gate, but my credentials checked out. I waited for another reporter from my company, Wes Brown. During the wait, a woman, Jade Garcia from CNN approached. She seemed like a friendly, young woman. She had never covered a story like this, and we chatted for a bit. Garcia, 26, had done extensive research on the inmates Arkansas planned to kill. She seemed confused about the rush to kill them.

As we talked, the media caravan began to move. The gates opened and a long procession of journalists made their way onto the road leading up to the ADC campus Execution Chamber. The line of vehicles began to move.

Once we passed the main gate, I saw a tall man standing in the distance. It was a man I knew well. Hunter Field, a reporter I had mentored at another newspaper, stood with a gaggle of reporters from the Arkansas Democrat Gazette. I made my way over to them. It was still hot, and the air buzzed. We talked for a bit, and then I decided to go inside. It was the first time I'd been in the facilities since I interviewed Echols in 2010. Media members were staged in one of the prison's mess halls. I sat down, pulled out my laptop, and began to read.

The waiting game began.

Another man, Death Row inmate Stacey Johnson was relieved that night. He was slated to die along with Lee, but the Arkansas Supreme Court ruled one day earlier that he should get an evidentiary hearing. His execution was stayed until the hearing could be held. His crimes are sinister.

...

Death knocked at Carol Heath's door.

The young mother of two let Stacey Johnson, into her De Queen-area apartment. Her daughter Ashley, 6, watched with her two-year-old brother Jonathan from an adjacent bedroom as a fight unfolded between the two. Ashley recalled the man visiting the apartment before. He seemed upset that her mother was dating another man. At one point, she saw her mother laying on the floor and bleeding. Johnson left. The children were too terrified to check on their mother.

Early the next morning, April 2, 1993, Heath's sister-in-law, Rose Cassidy, arrived at the apartment. Cassidy opened the unlocked door and made an appalling find. Heath's nude, blood covered body was on the floor. The only article of clothing on her body was a shirt that had been tied around her neck, concealing a deadly slash mark.

There was no semen recovered on or in the victim, but a condom box was found in the bathroom, and a douche bottle was also at the scene. A forensic pathologist testified later that if those items were used it would be difficult to recover any sperm.

The woman had several abrasions and bruises to her face, and defensive wounds on her hands. Bite marks and abrasions were found on her breasts. A hair from the killer was recovered on her body.

A few days later, the victim's purse was discovered in the woods between De Queen and the town of Horatio. A bloody pullover shirt, a bloody t-shirt, and bloody towel were found near the purse. Ashley told investigators the man in the house wore a green shirt. Johnson's stepmother told police she'd given him the shirts, which belonged to his father, to wear just prior to the murder. Forensic pathologists believe blood recovered from the green shirt matched Heath. Cigarette butts and other hairs were retrieved from the scene. Hairs found were a DNA match for Johnson.

Johnson first came to De Queen in January 1993 to attend his father's funeral. He stayed in town and met a man named Branson Ramsey. Heath was dating Ramsey. He attended a party at her apartment one night. After Ramsey left, Johnson remained and asked Heath and another woman if they would transport drugs for him and date him. The women refused. He made the same proposal a day later, and both women refused a second time.

Johnson was subsequently arrested in Albuquerque, N.M., about two weeks after the gruesome crime. He was convicted of capital murder and sentenced to die.

Since his conviction, Johnson has professed his innocence and asked for new DNA testing. New tests were performed and modern analysis showed an even stronger likelihood that his DNA was at the crime scene.

Ashley publicly stated she has forgiven Johnson and doesn't think he should die. Her brother, Jonathan, has said Johnson should die for the death of his mother. The ruling by the state's highest court gave Johnson a little more life.

As the hours passed Lee was going through the last motions of his life. The convicted killer refused a final, personal meal. He took communion instead. Moments later, he ate bread, chicken, rice, pinto beans, cinnamon rolls, and drank fruit punch from a standard issue prison food tray. Lee took a final shower. He dressed in all white clothes, and walked to a holding cell next to the Death Chamber. He huddled with his attorneys, hoping to receive a reprieve from the 8th Circuit Court of Appeals, or the U.S. Supreme Court. His execution was set to begin at 7 p.m.

A clock inside the media room slowly churned toward the appointed hour. Whenever a state official appeared and walked to a podium erected at the front of the room, media members dashed. Camera crews filmed, photographers snapped shots, and writers took notes. When the death hour came, the dull roar in the room turned into near silence. The two high courts issued stays until at least 8:30 p.m., and the waiting game renewed.

The hours ticked by. Darkness soon engulfed the prison complex. The gray, lifeless walls became a little darker. Journalists huddled in groups, exchanging jokes and notes. A film crew from the BBC interviewed different people, and filmed some of the conversations for a documentary the agency is producing about the death penalty. One journalist quipped this might be the only time in history that the U.S. Supreme Court held a direct grip on Arkansas. The statement was true. Newly appointed Justice Neil Gorsuch's first decisions on the high court would be the fates of death row inmates in Arkansas.

Lee's attorneys filed a slew of legal filings with the 8th Circuit Court of Appeals and the U.S. Supreme Court. His attorneys' arguments ranged from Lee's alleged mental incompetence to whether or not the lethal injection cocktail is humane.

A myriad of temporary stays and injunctions ensued. The night dragged on. Garcia openly wondered how the death penalty system operates. Lee's crimes were heinous she admitted, but he spent many hours that night, not knowing when the end would come, or if it would come at all.

"There has to be a better way of doing this," she said. "We should have a system … that is more dignified and orderly."

By 10 p.m., many of the veteran journalists in the room, confident earlier in the day Lee would die, now began to think he might have a chance to survive. Three media members, who volunteered to view the executions, remained in the room, a sign the executions might not take place.

I had not eaten all day. I tried to do a little fasted-cardio that day, and when I left my house there was no time to eat. Toward the back of the mess hall, a row of tables sat with pastries, water, fruit punch, and coffee. People gathered at the tables to snack and talk. Underneath the table, a large insect scampered. Above, on the wall, the clock continued its unabated march. After I saw the bug run from underneath the table, I lost my appetite. It did not even act as if it was scared of us.

"I guess he's seen scarier things in here than a bunch of reporters," an elderly man said who stood not far from me.

Around 11 p.m., the media witnesses were escorted to a staging area. It was at this time Lee and his legal team learned his stays had expired, and no injunction was forthcoming. The U.S. Supreme Court, in a 5-4 decision, decided to allow the execution to move forward. Gorsuch cast the deciding vote.

On my way into the complex, there were protestors outside, but as the hours went by, more and more had gathered outside. There were no reports of violence, but the crowd outside was extremely animated, according to the news reports I read. The fervor in the crowd grew as Lee was escorted into the Execution Chamber.

Lee didn't utter a single word in the moments before the lethal drug cocktail was injected into his body at 11:44 p.m. The 51-year-old remained stone-faced, and never made eye contact with Arkansas Department of Correction officials as they spoke the final words he would ever hear. He was strapped to a gurney and IVs were placed in his arms. Two phone calls were made to make sure there were not more legal issues to be decided. With the law satisfied,

Lee was asked not once, but twice if he had any final words.

His gaze remained straightforward. He never made eye contact with his questioner. Lee didn't publicly apologize for the heinous murders and rapes he committed. He offered no condolences to the grieving families.

At least 12 witnesses, two attorneys, and several ADC officials viewed the execution from the witness room. A few minutes in, an ADC official rubbed Lee's head and flicked his eyes to determine if he was incapacitated before potassium chloride, a heart-stopping drug was pumped into his body. He didn't show any signs he was awake. It was not divulged that night if any of Reese's family members viewed the execution. Media members reported the room was silent during the almost 12 minutes it took Lee to die. He was officially pronounced dead at 11:56 p.m., four minutes before his death warrant was set to expire.

He made no audible sounds, and from the vantage point of the witness room, he didn't appear to be in any noticeable discomfort, media representative Sean Murphy said.

"The inmate appeared to lose consciousness quickly," Murphy said.

State officials were pleased the execution was conducted without any issues.

"It is a very somber night for all Arkansans," Gov. Asa Hutchinson said. "At the end of the night the right thing was done ... the family of Debra Reese will have closure this evening."

Reese's family opted not to speak following Lee's death.

Protesters furiously erupted outside the prison. Paul Cates, communications director for the Innocence Project, which works to free wrongly accused inmates, issued a statement condemning the process.

"Ledell Lee proclaimed his innocence from the day of his arrest until the night of his execution, twenty-four years later," Cates said. "Arkansas's decision to rush through the execution of Mr. Lee just because its supply of lethal drugs are expiring at the end of the month denied him the opportunity to conduct DNA testing that could have proven his innocence. While reasonable people can disagree on whether death is an appropriate form of punishment, no one should be executed when there is a possibility that person is innocent."

Arkansas Attorney General Leslie Rutledge was glad the state was finally able to administer justice in the case. Lee was originally convicted in 1995.

"Tonight the lawful sentence of a jury which has been upheld by the courts through decades of challenges has been carried out. The family of the late Debra Reese, who was brutally murdered with a tire thumper after being targeted because she was home alone, has waited more than 24 years to see justice done. I pray this lawful execution helps bring closure for the Reese family."

Throughout the night, I had taken notes and written stories. I had enough information to write a complete story, but the media room was set to close. I said goodbye to Jade and Wes and walked to my car. The night was clear, and haunting. Police lights illuminated the sky. The road meandered through the fields surrounding the campus. Protestors continued to rally as I drove onto the main highway.

The lonely road to Little Rock awaited. The two-hour drive was solemn. I thought about Lee strapped to the gurney. I thought about his final thoughts. I thought about his victims and how he brutalized them. What were their last thoughts?

I stopped at a hotel, and wrote until the early morning. I had covered my first execution. It would not be my last. The next would make U.S. history.

Death Row Tales Part II

"An eye for an eye. A tooth for a tooth. A burn for a burn. A life for a life. Thats's how all this got started and that's how it will all end."

- Jenny Han

A little girl's dental appointment loomed, but Lacy Phillips would not visit the dentist on this day.

Her sister, Darla, dropped the 11-year-old off June 6, 1995, at the Automated Tax and Accounting Service in Bald Knob. Their mother, Mary Phillips, 34, worked as a bookkeeper. Her appointment was at 3 p.m. The mother of three hurried through her final tasks to leave on time. The family lived in the nearby town of Bradford, in White County. The rest of the family expected mother and daughter home by 4 p.m., but no later than 5 p.m.

A stranger suddenly appeared at the door.

The dark-haired man entered the building. He had come into the business earlier that day and asked to borrow tax information books. Jack Jones Jr., with a teardrop tattoo on his face, looked intently at mother and daughter. He complained he'd received the wrong books. Mary attempted to solve the problem. The situation immediately turned violent. He brandished a gun.

"Sorry … I'm going to have to rob you," he said.

He took them into a small break room. Jones told Mary to lie on her stomach, and he told Lacy to lie on top of her mother. It was the last moment the two would ever touch. He took the money out of the cash register. He asked if there was money in any other place. There wasn't. Jones tied Mary with a stereo speaker wire and placed her in a closet. He took Lacy into the bathroom. Jones meticulously tied her to a chair. He returned to the mother.

Mary's hands were tied with wire. Jones turned the woman around and wrapped a coffee pot cord around her neck. He violently anally raped her. How long the attack lasted is uncertain, but a medical examiner estimated she was choked for at least four minutes.

Her autopsy report indicated she had bruises, meaning she attempted to fight her attacker. She died from strangulation and blunt force trauma. It was likely the blunt force trauma wounds occurred before the strangulation, according to authorities. She might have been conscious for most of the attack. When Jones finished with the mother, he returned to the bathroom. Lacy, still bound and crying, begged him to not hurt her mother.

"I'm not … I'm here to hurt you," the killer told the girl.

He strangled Lacy until she fell unconscious. He beat her head with the butt of a BB gun. Blood splattered the space. The girl was struck eight times. After the vicious attack, Jones left the bathroom. He exited the business thinking the girl was dead. He wasn't alone in that thought. When police arrived, they thought she was dead, too. A photographer took pictures of the scene after police arrived. Mary was found nude from the waist down. As the photographer worked, Lacy suddenly opened her eyes. She had awakened before police arrived, but the sight of her own blood caused her to vomit and pass out a second time. Authorities rushed her to a nearby hospital. Lacy had lacerations and multiple skull fractures. Bone fragments penetrated her brain.

Miraculously, she survived.

She was able to identify Jones. Police officers went to Jones' home after the girl gave a detailed description of her attacker. The teardrop tattoo was the giveaway.

Jones admitted to police he killed the woman and tried to kill the girl. He told them he attacked the mother and daughter because he was mad at the police. His own wife had been raped, and the police did nothing, he said. It was the justification he used to rape and kill Mary Phillips and injure Lacy Phillips.

It took a jury 30 minutes to convict Jones in 1996. He was sentenced to death.

Jones' lawyers and relatives claimed through the years he suffers from depression and was abused both physically and sexually as a child. He was addicted to alcohol and drugs. His father was an alcoholic and his mother reportedly had serious gambling issues.

Days after his conviction, he asked the judge to "kill him immediately." His attorney, Jeff Rosenzweig of Little Rock, told the Arkansas Parole Board his client would not accept clemency if it were offered. He wanted to die, and he kept a picture of Lacy Phillips' battered body in his cell as a reminder of what he did, according to numerous published reports.

"I keep it so I would never forget to remember," the 52-year-old said.

The murder of Mary Phillips and the attempted murder of Lacy were not the first diabolical crimes committed by Jones.

Police found Lorraine Anne Barrett, 32, murdered June 1, 1991, inside a Days Inn hotel room in Fort Lauderdale, Florida. Investigators discovered she had been in the Elbow Room, a local bar, the same night she checked into the hotel. Barrett was seen with a white male that night. Witnesses told police about a series of tattoos the male had. The two were seen at the bar and in a hotel elevator. Barrett, a Pennsylvania native was reportedly on vacation.

Barrett was strangled to death, and DNA was recovered from the crime scene. Despite a composite sketch of the suspect, the case went cold. A detective in 2002 reopened the case and the DNA collected was placed in the National DNA Indexing System (NDIS). It matched Jones. He was subsequently charged and convicted of Barrett's murder.

Jones languished on Arkansas's Death Row for years, and in the spring 2017, he finally got his wish. Arkansas Gov. Asa Hutchinson set his execution date – April 24.

Arkansas planned a double execution that night, the first in the U.S. in more than 17 years. I made a second trip to southern Arkansas. Little did I know I would cross paths with Lacy. I asked her one question that night.

It was one of the toughest questions I've ever asked.

The trip south was just as hot as the previous one. Springtime in Arkansas is beautiful, but when the heat and humidity set in, it can be miserable. I was better prepared for this temporary road trip to Death Row. As I drove, I wondered if Jones would die that night, and I wondered if the other man sentenced to death, murderer and rapist Marcel Williams, would be spared by the court of appeals or even the U.S. Supreme Court. His crimes are unforgiveable.

...

Stacy Errickson, 22, decided to drive herself to work and the decision cost the mother of two her life. Errickson usually car-pooled with a friend, but on Nov. 20, 1994, she drove her own vehicle. She stopped at a Jacksonville gas station. A man approached. Two other women would later tell police about the same man menacing them around the same time.

Marcel Williams brandished a firearm and made Errickson move to the passenger seat. They stopped at ATM machines and he forced her to withdraw $350. The last attempted transaction was at 7:37 a.m. Errickson never arrived at work. She never picked her children up from the babysitter.

Her body was found in a shallow grave at a nearby park almost a month later. She had been raped and strangled. Police initially interviewed Williams Nov. 29, 1994, more than two weeks before her body was found. He admitted to police he abducted her, but told them he only robbed her. As far as he knew, she was still alive, and he didn't sexually assault her.

After her body was found, he was charged with capital murder, robbery, and rape. He was convicted. Williams, now 46, was sentenced to death. For years, attorneys argued he should have only received a life term.

Jurors were never told about his violent upbringing. Jurors, according to legal precedent, must consider mitigating factors, such as abuse a defendant might have endured as an adolescent. His original attorneys never raised the fact he had been sexually and physically abused to the jury.

Maybe one of these factors would sway judges to spare his life.

When I arrived, the frenzied atmosphere was much more subdued. Far less media members attended, and there were no protesters there that I noticed. I stepped into the parking lot. I was angry and looking to confront another journalist who had covered the first execution. A few days before, I had written a story about journalist Jade Garcia covering Lee's execution for CNN.

This other journalist, who I will not name, blasted me in a comments section online. He made several accusations about the story, including a commentary on my description of the media room before the execution, and then he insinuated Garcia wasn't there or didn't exist. Several online viewers flooded him with Garcia's social media accounts, including Facebook, Twitter, and others. They eviscerated his maligned comments. Her work for CNN was easy to find.

I found out about his comments as I drove through the gates of the ADC campus. I was furious. If he were there, I would have confronted him. He was not there, and I did call him several days later. We had a very candid conversation, and he apologized.

Jones' execution was a certainty. It was slated for 7 p.m. The hour approached. The lethal injection was a go.

Media members were escorted to the viewing room. The sun began to descend in the sky. Witnesses prepared for the second execution in days. Jones did enjoy a last meal. He ate fried chicken, potato logs with tartar sauce, beef jerky, a Butterfinger candy bar, a milkshake, and fruit punch.

Medical staffers spent 45 minutes attempting to place a central line in his neck. Jones suffered from diabetes and was obese, according to the staff. The line had to be placed in another part of his body.

Before the procedure started, Jones spoke. Jones said he "loved Lacy like his own child." He delivered a calm, but at times, rambling statement.

"I just want to let the family and Lacy know how sorry I am. I cannot believe I did something to her. I tried to be respectful from the time I took and become a better person. I hope I did better," Jones said. "I hope over time you could learn who I really am, and I am not a monster. There was a reason why those things happened that day. I am so sorry Lacy, try to understand I love you like my own child."

Jones also composed a written statement.

"I want people to know that when I came to prison I made up my mind that I would be a better person when I left than when I came in. I had no doubt in my mind that I would make every effort to do this. I would like to think that I've accomplished this. I've made every effort to be a good person – I practiced Buddhism and studied physics. I met the right people and did the right things. There are no words that would fully express my remorse for the pain I caused," he said.

Moments later he received a toxic drug cocktail at 7:06 p.m. He was declared dead at 7:20 p.m. Witnesses stated he did not appear to be in any visible pain during the execution. His wish and the wishes of his victims' family had finally been carried out.

Gov. Hutchinson issued a statement following the execution.

"This evening the rule of law was upheld when the sentence of the jury for Jack Jones was carried out after 20 years of review. The victim's family has waited patiently for justice during that time. The jury sentenced Jack Jones to death, and his sentence was upheld by judges and reviewed thoroughly in courts of appeal at each level.

"A governor never asks for this responsibility, but I accept it as part of the solemn pledge I made to uphold the law.

Jack Jones expressed his willingness to proceed today, and we hope this will help bring closure to the Phillips family."

After the execution, we got a surprise visit in the media room. Family members, including Lacy, appeared to make a statement and take a question or two. I stood with a gaggle of reporters near the podium where they were slated to speak. As she stood there, I knew I had to ask her the question that was on everyone's mind, but no one wanted to ask.

I spoke.

"Jack Jones said he considers you a daughter and that he loves you. What are your thoughts on that?" I asked her. It was obvious she was stunned by the question and took a visible step backwards as the words came out of my mouth. She quickly collected herself with words.

"I don't want to talk about that ... I'm glad it's done ... that chapter is closed," she said.

She held hands with family members during the brief meeting. At least 12 family members attended the press conference. Some viewed the execution. Her father, James Phillips was defiant about how long it took to execute Jones.

"I hope the state of Arkansas learns from this," he said. "It don't take 22 years to get something done."

Mary Phillips' son, Jesse James Phillips, said he didn't want to talk about Jones or his death. He wanted to focus on his mother who died when he was 14.

"I don't dwell on how she was taken from me," he said. "No events from today will bring her back."

Jones was done. Williams' wait would last most of the night. I pounded away on my laptop as Williams' final appeals trickled through the courts. Diabetic and weighing about 400 pounds, his attorneys argued the state's lethal injection methods would cause him more pain than an average inmate. Williams could not have the central line placed in his body due to his size and medical condition. It meant he would be more prone to suffering and torture, his attorneys argued.

He was originally slated to die at 8:15 p.m. but a temporary stay was granted so cruel and unusual punishment arguments could be vetted. Williams' odyssey that night was intense.

The first time Williams was escorted into the Death Chamber, he looked straightforward and never peered outside as twilight canvassed the sky for the final time in his life. He was strapped to the gurney for an undisclosed amount of time, according to media witnesses. Witnesses were moved from the viewing room to a waiting van. Before leaving the room, the words "I'm not letting you out" emanated from the Death Chamber where Williams was restrained. ADC officials confirmed that during the stay, Williams was allowed to use the restroom back in his cell. A short time later, witnesses were escorted back into the room.

At 10:16 p.m., the curtains in the viewing room were lifted. Williams was restrained with IVs in his right arm. Williams only shook his head "no" when asked if he wanted to give a final statement. Soon after, drugs were pumped into his body. During the first few minutes, Williams continued to breathe heavily. His eyes closed, but the right eye remained slightly opened throughout the entire procedure. His lips appeared to grimace at one point, AP News Editor Kelly Kissel noted.

"I didn't get the sense it was discomfort," he said.

Media witnesses reported a possible second dose of sedative was given to Williams a little more than five minutes after the execution began. By 10:24 p.m., Williams didn't appear to be breathing. He was officially declared dead at 10:33 p.m.

His attorneys argued after the fact that Williams suffered during his execution. They argued that he "moved his lips" and at one point "gulped for air." Media witnesses noticed he moved his lips slightly after he was asked to give his final statement.

It was done. The first double execution in the U.S. in nearly two decades was completed. I left the ADC campus. Once again, it was late night.

As I drove in the darkness, my mind was consumed with life and death. I thought about Lacy and the horror she suffered as a little girl. I thought about the horrors Jones' suffered before he turned into a murderous monster. I wondered what went through Williams mind in the moments before he died. Did he have remorse for what he had done? I also wondered what went through Stacy's mind while that animal raped and killed her.

Human beings can be extremely depraved.

I drove about two hours north to Little Rock. I spent several hours writing through the wee hours of the morning. I slept for a few hours and then made the drive home. I stopped at a restaurant to eat. Two men sat near me talking about the executions. One had a copy of the USA Today in his hands. There was a story about the executions.

It was weird listening to others speculate about something I witnessed and wrote about. As journalists, we often forget about the impact we have on other people's lives, and the historic things we witness, firsthand.

Arkansas had only one inmate left to execute, Kenneth Williams. He was slated to die April 27, 2017. He was the most controversial, in my estimation, of the four men who were ultimately executed that April. There were many people who thought Kenneth Williams was mentally impaired, and that should be grounds to spare his life. The details of his crimes are unforgettable, and made national news.

...

Genie Boren knew something was amiss when she walked into her Grady-area home. The place had been ransacked. Guns owned by the family were gone, and so was her 57-year-old husband, Cecil, who had been working in the garden when she left.

Frantic, she called a neighbor, Kay McLemore. The two began to search. They found Cecil face down in a nearby bayou. The father and husband had been shot seven times and wasn't wearing socks or shoes. No one knows if he begged for mercy, or attempted to fight his attacker. Scrape marks on his body indicated he had been dragged to the spot. A pool of blood near the home indicated where the shooting took place. His killer, escaped convicted murderer Kenneth Williams, took the man's clothes, money, guns, rings, and truck after he stole Cecil's life.

Williams headed north. In Missouri, he got into a high-speed chase with law officers. During the chase that spanned almost 60 miles starting in Lebanon, Mo., Williams drove at speeds of more than 120 miles per hour. He struck another vehicle, killing the driver, Michael Greenwood. After police arrested him following a short pursuit on foot, Williams reportedly spat at Greenwood's body and blamed him for his failed escape attempt as he was escorted by officers near the man's body. He was wearing two of Cecil Boren's rings when he was arrested, and was wearing his victim's clothes.

He had been apprehended one day after the killing, on Oct. 4, 1999. He was convicted of capital murder and sentenced to death.

"The meeting of my brothers and sisters when we get together, it will never be the same," Cecil's sister, Annette Boren Knight, said to jurors at Williams' sentencing. "We ask ourselves, what we can do in situations like this? Well, we cannot do anything as a family but hold together and pray together ... you can do something ... what would you do if it was your brother, or your sister, or your baby that someone stole away from you? I can't do anything, but you can."

Williams' Death Row journey began when he killed a college student Dec. 13, 1998. On that day, Williams approached two college students, Peter Robertson and Dominique Hurd, a cheerleader at the University of Arkansas at Pine Bluff, in a restaurant parking lot in Pine Bluff. He pointed a gun at the students and kidnapped them. He directed the couple to an ATM machine where he stole $70 from Robertson's account.

He ordered them to drive down several dead-end streets. At one point, he told the couple to exit the car and forced Robertson to take pictures of Hurd after Williams removed her underwear. They drove down another dead-end street, and he ordered them to climb a fence and kneel behind a shed. He was about to drive away when he stopped and opened fire on the couple. Hurd was killed.

After his first-degree murder conviction in Hurd's murder, Williams was transported to the Cummins Unit in Grady. The morning he killed Cecil Boren, Williams was released from the barracks around 7 a.m. to conduct a religious prayer. The designated prayer place was near the prison kitchens. He escaped inside a slop tank filled with food scraps. The normal tank had a gate on it, but it had a flat tire that morning. The reserve tank didn't have a gate. Within a mile of the Boren home, Williams jumped out of the tank, and hid in a ditch. He removed his prison garb and soon encountered Cecil. The flat tire cost the man his life.

Williams also confessed to an unrelated murder. In 2005, he sent a letter to the Pine Bluff Commercial Appeal, a local newspaper. In the letter, he said the same day he killed Hurd he shot and killed 36-year-old Jerrell Jenkins during a robbery. A student found his body in a ditch. The case was unsolved until the letter.

Despite his crimes, there were many who tried to sway Gov. Asa Hutchinson to commute his sentence.

European Union Ambassador to the U.S., David O' Sullivan, sent the governor a letter asking him to spare the convicted killer's life. He expressed sympathy for the victims and their families, but he argued executing Williams would be inhumane.

"I believe this evidence should be heard and that Mr. Williams should not be executed," he said. "We believe that the elimination of the death penalty is fundamental to the protection of human dignity, and to the progressive development of human rights on a global scale. Furthermore, we are convinced that applying the death penalty will have no deterrent effect."

He continued:

"This unprecedented pace of carrying out those sentences has been justified by the urge to use some of the execution drugs before their expiration dates. We also note with concern that other drugs used for executions were reportedly acquired by circumventing the policies of the company who sold them. Proceeding with Mr. Williams' execution would therefore be a very concerning precedent."

Attorneys asked state officials to allow Kayla Greenwood, the daughter of victim Michael Greenwood, and Stacey

Yaw, the widow, an opportunity to testify at the Arkansas Parole Board in support of Mr. Williams's clemency.

"In her letter, Ms. Greenwood explained that if she had known about Mr. Williams request for clemency, her family would have requested to testify at the hearing on behalf of Mr. Williams and would have asked the board to grant clemency," her attorneys stated. "While acknowledging that Mr. Williams' actions from nearly twenty years ago caused her family considerable pain, she believes that executing Mr. Williams would only cause them 'additional suffering.'"

Hutchinson was not moved.

"I have reviewed the letter from the Greenwood family, and I appreciate the genuine spirit of forgiveness and compassion demonstrated by Ms. Greenwood. Her letter certainly has an impact; however, my responsibility is to look at the totality of the case including the view of all the victims and the interest of justice. Kenneth Williams murdered multiple people, and actions have consequences. Kenneth Williams murdered 19-year-old Nikki Hurd and was charged with capital murder. Williams was then spared the death penalty by the jury who gave him life in prison without the possibility of parole. Despite this showing of mercy, Kenneth Williams determined to escape from prison. After 18 days in prison, he escaped and took human life again with the killing of Cecil Boren. These facts support the final verdict of the second jury in giving the death penalty."

The execution moved forward April 27, but I was not there. Our reporter, Wes Brown, covered it. My daughter's softball team was competing in a tournament, and even though I'd written about Kenneth Williams prior to his execution, I was off the proverbial hook. Throughout the night, I did keep tabs with Wes to see what was happening. It became clear the courts and the governor would not save the Death Row inmate.

When his appeals failed, it was time for Kenneth Williams to die. Williams read a statement to the family and his victims, while also announcing himself as a "Death-Row preacher."

"I was more than wrong. The crimes I perpetrated against you all were senseless, extremely hurtful, and inexcusable. I humbly beg for your forgiveness and pray you find the peace, healing, and closure you all deserve," Williams read. "I am not the same person I was. I have been transformed. Some things cannot be undone. I seek forgiveness."

Just before his execution began, Williams was reported to have spoken in tongues. The execution began at 10:55 p.m. Each execution begins with an injection of midazolam to render the prisoner unconscious. Vecuronium bromide is then injected to paralyze the inmate, and then potassium chlorid is injected to stop the heart. When his execution was completed, ADC officials released a statement saying Williams shook for about 10 seconds during the start of the procedure.

Media witnesses painted a different picture.

Media members stated he convulsed 15 to 20 times. He gasped several times, and continued to make sounds four minutes after the procedure started. Media members observed "coughing, convulsing, lurching, jerking with sound." Once the shaking subsided, prison medical personnel performed a consciousness check. His eyelids were examined and his chest was massaged. Medical personnel determined he was unconscious.

Williams' attorneys released a scathing statement.

"Attorneys for Mr. Williams have no doubt that he suffered an extremely painful death based on what they personally witnessed. They have also stated that because all of the prisoners were paralyzed during their executions over the past eight days, they cannot know whether Marcel Williams, Jack Jones, and Ledell Lee 'were not also consciously suffocating.'"

The statements went further.

"The accounts of the execution of Mr. Williams tonight are horrifying. We tried repeatedly to get the state to comport with their own protocol to avoid torturing our client to death, and yet reports from the execution witnesses indicate that Mr. Williams suffered during this execution. Press reports state that within three minutes into the execution, our client began coughing, convulsing, jerking, and lurching with sound that was audible even with the microphone turned off. This is very disturbing, but not at all surprising, given the history of the risky sedative midazolam, which has been used in many botched executions. What is important right now is that all the information about tonight's execution must be meticulously documented and preserved so that we can discover exactly what happened in that execution chamber. The courts were wrong for not intervening. Gov. Hutchinson's spokesman, who commented that our client experienced "involuntary muscular reactions," is simply trying to whitewash the reality of what happened. We are requesting a full investigation into tonight's problematic execution," attorney Shawn Nolan said.

A federal judge ordered blood and sample tissues to be taken following his controversial execution. As of this writing, nothing has occurred as a result of the ruling. The executions were finished.

Government executions have always vexed me. Many on Death Row would rather die than languish for the rest of their lives in prison, and it bothers me that the government has the power to kill its own citizens. On the other hand, I interview and write about the victims and their families. The pain they feel can't be described. This is one issue that I can change my mind about on a daily, if not hourly, basis at times. One thing was for sure after Williams was executed.

My short stay on Death Row finally ended.

Karen Johnson Swift

"Sometimes you will never know the value of a moment until it becomes a memory."

- Dr. Seuss

Karen Johnson Swift was ready to have some fun.

Her life had been stress filled in the weeks leading up to Oct. 29, 2011. It was a Saturday night, and a Halloween party was being held at a local country club in Dyersburg, Tennessee. Karen, along with a female friend, decided to attend. Karen's eldest daughter, Ashley, was staying the night with friends. They went to the party.

Less than three weeks before, Karen had filed for divorce from her husband, David Swift. The couple had two college age children, Preston and Dustin, and another daughter, Keeley. They had been divorced previously, but had reconciled and remarried. Now, the relationship had taken another turn, but the couple still lived in the same home they shared with their two grade-school age daughters.

After the party, the two women went to a McDonald's and bought fries. They were either at the friend's home or on their way when Karen got a text message from Ashley. Her daughter wanted to come home. Karen obliged her child. She gathered Ashley and headed to the Swift home. Mother and daughter went to sleep in the same bed around 2 a.m., according to Dyer County Sheriff Jeff Box.

Little did the girl know it would be the last moment she would ever spend with her mother.

Sometime after that, Karen Swift vanished. There were few reported clues as to what happened to her. David Swift was home when Karen and Ashley arrived. Police said he was the last person to speak with her.

A motorist noticed something odd along the road hours after Karen fell asleep with Ashley. Her 2004 Nissan Murano was parked about a mile from the house. It had a flat tire. There were no signs of a struggle inside the vehicle, police said. Her Halloween costume was in the car. The only thing missing was the 44-year-old. A shirt and a pair of jeans belonging to the woman was found near her vehicle, according to reports. Police would later deny any of her DNA was found on the clothes.

I was a journalist working at a newspaper in Northeast Arkansas when I received several calls about Karen's disappearance. The Swift family was from NEA. The family moved to Dyersburg a couple of years before so that David Swift could take a job. Karen was a 1985 Walnut Ridge High School graduate.

The number of calls and the intensity from the people I spoke with led me to the conclusion that Karen was well-liked in the community. At the time, I thought something sinister may have happened to her, but I also thought she might have just walked away from her life.

I made a few calls, and was able to get a hold of her son, Dustin. He was extremely distraught. A freshman at the University of Tennessee at Martin, he had been angry with his mother in the weeks leading up to the disappearance. He was upset about the pending divorce. Choking back tears, he told me she tried to text him several times before that night, and he wouldn't return them because he was upset. His father notified him about his mother's disappearance a few hours after her vehicle was discovered. Shocked, he immediately drove to Dyersburg.

"I didn't even grab my clothes – I didn't think. I just left," he told me.

The divorce had clouded his judgment.

"That's what hurts the most right now," he said. "When she told me about the divorce, it hurt. I feel so guilty because I wouldn't text her back."

When the conversation turned to his mother possibly being abducted, his tone changed. His mother was an athletic woman who played sports. She was a fixture at the baseball fields in Pocahontas, their former hometown, when Preston and Dustin played. She was feisty and would have been hard to subdue, he said.

"I know her really well … she would definitely fight for her life," he said. Later, he added he had "A lot of faith that she is still alive."

Friends and family swarmed Dyersburg in the days that followed. Candlelight vigils were held. High school classmate Janet Ross told me Karen was a Teacher's Pet in school and was well liked by her classmates. She was kind of shy and reserved in school, but blossomed after she graduated.

"I keep calling her cell phone, hoping she'll eventually answer," Ross said. "It's a nightmare that won't end."

Another friend, Holly Sutton, drove to Dyersburg. When she arrived, she was numbed when she saw police and searchers combing the area near where her vehicle was found. Sutton said Karen spent most of her free time with her children and their activities. Karen was an active gardener. Sutton dismissed any notion that Karen willfully left. Her kids meant too much to her.

"She was a full-time mother who really loved her kids," Sutton said. "They were everything to her."

Another person that knew Karen was former high school counselor Joyce Rose. I've known Joyce and her family for many years, and I wanted her insights about Karen. Joyce was baffled by the disappearance. She remembered Karen as a nice kid, who spent most of her time with her children after she became an adult. The entire episode was strange, she said.

"Karen grew into a beautiful young mother," she said. "We're just shocked by this. It doesn't make sense."

During the first few days of the search, one of the Swifts' neighbors was arrested for poisoning their dog and another dog a month earlier. David Swift reported to police on Oct. 7, 2011, he observed their dog near the neighbor's property, and when the animal returned it fell ill. The family took the dog to the veterinarian's office. Karen went to the man's house to talk with him about the incident, and noticed a blue substance in a pan. Another neighbor reported that his or her dog died after visiting the same property.

Box said his office received evidence of the animal poisoning from the crime lab the same week, and the arrest was coincidental, and the neighbor was not involved in her disappearance.

Days turned into weeks, and the police released almost no information. I called Sheriff Box dozens of times. Dyersburg was more than an hour's drive, so I couldn't visit his office. His refusal to answer phone calls irritated me. I got numerous other calls from people claiming to have information about Karen. One private detective claimed he had information that Karen was part of a high society sex ring and that she had been killed to keep her quiet. I never found any evidence to support this theory.

Another person called and claimed Karen was abducted and killed by a serial killer targeting women with blue eyes and blonde hair in western Tennessee. This person said it was the same killer that took a young woman, 20-year-old Holly Bobo on April 13, 2011.

Holly was a nursing student. She woke early that morning at her parent's house in Parsons, Tennessee. Around 7:30 a.m., a neighbor heard a scream, and dogs started to bark.

Holly's brother, Clint, noticed a camouflaged clothed man talking to his sister in the yard. He thought it was her boyfriend, Drew Scott. The two appeared to be arguing. At one point he heard the words "No" and "Why" uttered by his sister. It looked as if the two were breaking up and the male did most of the talking, he said.

His mother, Karen Bobo, called the house as this unfolded outside. She became immediately alarmed. Drew Scott was turkey hunting and the man was not Holly's boyfriend, she told Clint. The mother ordered her son to retrieve a gun and shoot the man. Clint was confused because he still thought the man was her boyfriend. Holly and the man soon disappeared into a patch of nearby woods. Clint quickly realized the man was larger than his sister's boyfriend. He got a gun. There was blood splatter in the garage. DNA tests confirmed it was Holly's

Holly's mother called police at 8 a.m. The search for her began. Her cell phone pinged several times after that, but it didn't lead authorities to her. Holly Bobo, a blonde haired, blue-eyed girl was missing. Stories and allegations swirled.

There were claims Clint killed his sister. He was polygraphed and passed the test. Others thought the mother's immediate reaction to tell her son to shoot the man meant she knew his identity and knew what he was there to do. The Tennessee Bureau of Investigation handled the case. Many thought it was botched from the beginning, and at one point it was rumored she was an undercover informant and she was killed by law enforcement. This theory gained steam because Holly seemed to comply with the stranger's request for her to walk into the woods.

These theories proved false. As many as six people were arrested in the case, on varying charges that changed almost daily at one point. The TBI and prosecutors were under intense pressure as the case unfolded, and many mistakes were made. The case garnered worldwide attention. Her cousin, country music star Whitney Duncan, made several public pleas for information.

In 2014, a ginseng hunter made a grisly discovery in Decatur County, not far from the Bobo home. A human skull, teeth, and other bone remnants were scattered in the woods. Her panties, cellphone, and lunchbox where also recovered during the investigation. The hunter prayed it was part of science set and not real. It was what remained of Holly Bobo. Her body was found near the last cell phone tower her cell phone pinged. It was six miles from Zachary Adams' house.

Adams, along with his brother, John "Dylan" Adams, and two other men, Shayne Austin, and Jason Autry were implicated in the murder. The story that emerged was devastating.

Jason Autry, testified at Zachary Adams's murder trial in September 2017, that Adams bragged to him how he, his brother, and Austin drugged Holly, and then ganged raped her. The men took turns raping the young woman in a barn, according to his version of events. Autry, a drug addict, came to Adams' house to get drugs the morning of the kidnapping and assault. When he arrived, Adams told him he needed help "taking care of a problem."

Holly was wrapped in a blanket in the back of Adams' truck. The two men assumed she was dead, and planned to dump her in a nearby river. Adams and Autry planned to "gut her" meaning they would remove her internal organs to ensure her body wouldn't float to the surface. When they arrived at the waterway, Holly moaned or moved. Adams shot her in the head, killing her. The two men panicked, thinking someone heard the gunshot, and they drove away before finishing their ghoulish plan.

How Holly ended up in the woods remains a mystery.

The gun reportedly used to kill Holly was located, and Adams' then girlfriend said he bragged about the killing. He even threatened to do the same thing to her if she didn't obey him. Despite a complete lack of DNA or forensic evidence, Adams was convicted and sentenced to life in prison. His brother entered an Alford plea and was sentenced to 35 years in prison. He gave a jumbled and inaccurate confession to authorities. Austin was never charged with murder, and was offered immunity in the case if he could lead police to the woman's body. He could not and reportedly committed suicide in a Florida hotel room in 2015.

This case is extremely odd. I am inclined to think investigators did a poor job in this case, but the brothers are likely involved. In the absence of new evidence, it is hard to argue against the prosecution's case. The two men and their mother have professed their innocence from the beginning. There is one thing I'm sure about. I doubt this case is linked to the Karen Johnson Swift case.

Those long weeks turned into a month. Thanksgiving came and went and there was no sign of Karen. The search expanded to areas around Obion River and White Lake near Dyersburg. Box continued to dodge my calls for information, but local media in Dyersburg reported that he said no major evidence was found during these searches.

The case changed Dec. 10, 2011. Karen's decomposed body was found underneath kudzu bushes in or near an abandoned cemetery a few miles from her home. Two men were in the cemetery examining broken tombstones when they noticed what appeared to be an arm or leg in the kudzu. Cold weather had killed part of the kudzu bushes revealing her body.

She was identified through her dental records, Sheriff Box told me afterwards. Her body was in such bad condition specialized forensic experts had to be brought in to examine her, and it was almost a month before her family could bury her.

Police have not released the cause of death, and whether she had been sexually assaulted has never been divulged. Box said shortly after her body had been found there were no outward signs of a sexual attack. Her body had been intentionally placed in the spot where it was found. There was no way, she wandered to that spot and died. This was clearly a homicide case, police said.

Intense media scrutiny was difficult to deal with, but the sheriff said at the time he would not reveal too much. The autopsy was sealed through a court order. Box stopped talking to the media entirely, and all media inquiries were sent to prosecutors. As expected, prosecutors were not forthcoming with information, either.

Once Karen had been buried, the focus turned to the investigation. Her husband, David Swift, was not identified as a suspect by authorities. Box told me David Swift was cooperative with police and he allowed his daughter that fell asleep with her mother in the early morning hours prior to Karen's death to be interviewed by detectives. If the police developed any leads at this time, none of the new information was shared with the public.

...

Time slowly passed, I had to move on to other stories. The year 2012 was a big one. It was a presidential election year with incumbent President Barack Obama locked in a tight battle with Republican Mitt Romney. I have always covered national, state, and local political stories, and they are among my favorites.

Hurricane Sandy struck the east coast. The monster storm took lives and caused billions in damage. I've written a lot about hurricanes, and the after math, too. There was one gut-wrenching story that stole national headlines and it hit close to home.

A 20-year-old man, Adam Lanza, stood outside the Sandy Hook Elementary School on Dec. 14, 2012, in Newtown, Connecticut. He was wearing black fatigues, a bulletproof vest and had three guns, including a semi-automatic AR-15. Hours earlier, he killed his own mother, Nancy Lanza. He shot his way into the locked-down school.

Bullets rained in the hallway as he made his way to his first classroom. A group of young children were in class when the killer entered. He slaughtered the students in the room. He entered a second classroom and continued his killing spree. Police arrived at the school minutes after the shooting started. Lanza killed himself, after murdering 20 students and six adults. All the children murdered were either in first or second grade. It was the worse school shooting in U.S. history.

I didn't cover Sandy Hook, but it reopened an old, bitter wound in Northeast Arkansas. A little more than 14 years prior to Sandy Hook, one of the worst school shootings in the country's history happened on the Westside School District campus March 24, 1998, in Jonesboro. I wrote about this incident several times years after it happened. I knew some of the teachers, police, and even journalists that were there on that terrible day.

It started when the fire alarm sounded at the Westside Middle School.

A student, 11-year-old Andrew Golden, was dressed in camouflage when he walked into the school to trigger the alarm around 12:30 p.m. A student saw him do it, and told his teacher it was a prank. The fire alarm procedures still had to be followed. Golden would surely be punished, afterward. Students were led to the schoolyard. The district had just finished spring break, and the last nine weeks of the school year had begun. It was a mild, sunny day, and death was on its way.

Golden and his friend, 13-year-old Mitchell Johnson, were lying in wait. They had a perfect view of their unsuspecting victims filling the schoolyard. The two had skipped school that day to initiate their deadly plot. The two started firing rounds at the gathered students. A hail of bullets fell from the sky. At first, many thought it was just firecrackers. But then, students started to fall. Teachers stepped in front of their kids to shield them from the onslaught.

Janna Berry, a third-year educator at the school, sat in the teacher's lounge as the alarm sounded. When she arrived outside, she thought students were playing with fireworks on the other side of the building. She and a football coach set out to stop the rambunctious students. Horrified faces, screams, and badly injured children met them as they rounded the corner.

Sixth-grade English teacher Shannon Wright threw student Emma Pitman out of the way. Seconds later the young mother was shot; she later died. Shannon was 32. Four students — Natalie Brooks, 11, Stephanie Johnson, 12, Britthney Varner,11, and Paige Herring, 12 — perished under a hail of gunfire. A few were still alive when medics arrived but later died at the hospital. Ballistics tests later confirmed Golden killed Paige, Natalie, and Britthney. Johnson killed the teacher and he was the likely gunman that killed Stephanie, according to police.

Ten others were seriously injured. Among them was Candice Porter, an 11-year-old who reportedly dated Johnson for a couple of days and then broke up with him before the attack. Golden's ex-girlfriend, 12-year-old Jennifer Jacobs was shot. They'd recently split up.

One girl was sprawled on the sidewalk near Janna as she rushed into the madness. Bullets riddled her body. She and another teacher held the little girl until she died. Nothing could be done to save her life. Her injuries were too severe. Janna declined to identify the child during our interview out of respect for the girl's family, and I totally respect her for not divulging the child's identity.

Students were steered to the perceived safety of the gym. Only one of the shooting victims was male; many of the male classmates were in gym class when the alarm was pulled, which might be why 14 girls were shot. The entire episode lasted two minutes. An estimated 30 rounds were fired.

The gunmen fled, but one of them almost did not. Golden didn't move in the moments after the shooting, and Johnson admitted in a court deposition he put a pistol against the boy's head and told him to run. Johnson and Golden were apprehended as they fled to a van filled with food and camping supplies.

Brandi Varner, Britthney's sister, said in 2006 that her sister had a crush on Golden since the two were in first grade. Britthney called Golden during spring break, the week before the shootings, her sister said.

Journalist Curt Hodges was on his lunch break when he noticed a fleet of emergency vehicles headed toward the school. He called the police, and they told him about the shooting. I worked with Curt for several years, and he's one of the best story-telling journalists I've ever worked with. We talked several times about his experience that day.

"I jumped into my car and drove straight out there," Hodges said.

Bloodstained sidewalks, bewildered students, and screams met the veteran journalist. Car after car careened into the ditches near the school. Frantic parents and other relatives exited their vehicles and raced into the school to find loved ones, Hodges told me. The dying and the dead littered the ground. Curt was the first media member on the scene.

"I'll never forget that," Hodges said.

Hodges drove back to his office and filed the first story to hit The Associated Press wire detailing the massacre. Media from around the world descended on Northeast Arkansas to cover what was arguably the second-worst public school shooting in U.S. history — the only comparison was the Stockton schoolyard shooting in 1989, in which five children were killed, 29 children and a teacher were wounded, and the gunman shot himself.

Word soon spread to the elementary and high schools on the Westside campus. Meagan Cremeens, then a fourth-grader, was in class when a call went over the loudspeaker asking teachers to bring their earthquake emergency response kits to the office. Her teacher told the class about the shooting. Meagan's mind quickly went to her sister, Brittany, who was in the middle school. She drew a picture of Brittany and prayed, "Please don't let it be her."

Hours later Meagan's father picked her up. They found her sister, unharmed.

To this day, no one knows the true motives behind the shooting. Johnson and Golden were juveniles at the time, which meant they couldn't be charged as adults. Much of what they said to police and in court has been sealed.

"I wasn't intentionally aiming for anyone ... it was never planned on my behalf to harm anyone," Johnson said in a civil court deposition released in 2007. "I didn't go to the school that day to kill anyone."

The shooters were about 100 yards from their victims, which means it would have been difficult to target certain people, but not impossible, ballistics experts say. Rumors swirled the break-ups and problems with teachers spurred the attack. In the weeks leading up to the shooting, Johnson bragged to classmates about his alleged gang ties.

Johnson and Golden stole a cache of guns from relatives hours before the shooting. Golden first broached the idea to Johnson around Christmas in 1997.

In one interview years after the fact, Johnson claimed he couldn't remember what happened that day and insisted that he never fired directly at people — even though ballistics tests showed otherwise. He was remorseful for shooting his teacher.

"Mrs. Wright was always good to me ...," he said. "Mrs. Wright was a good woman."

One image haunted him. He watched Golden fire the shot that took Natalie Brooks' life. Johnson considered her a friend. Golden and Johnson were incarcerated at a juvenile detention facility for the maximum term allowed by law — imprisonment until age 21. Johnson was released in 2005. Golden was released two years later.

Johnson has since been sent to federal prison for drugs and credit card fraud. Johnson lives in Houston now, and Golden has moved several times after his release from juvenile detention. They are the only two mass school shooters in U.S. history that are free.

I talked to several mothers of the victims through the years. Most family members involved in this attack don't like to talk about it. I thought it was ironic that students protesting the increase in school shootings chose March 24, 2018, to hold protests nation and worldwide following a wave of mass shootings across the country. It was ironic to me because in the coverage I never heard Westside mentioned much. I read one column in the New York Times.

The year 2012 came and went and nothing significant happened with the Karen Swift case. One interesting aspect of the case was David Swift. He was never named a suspect and from everything I'd read, to that point, and he had cooperated fully in the investigation. I was told there was tension because her family did suspect him of involvement. I briefly talked to him on the phone after the murder. He was cordial, but didn't offer any details.

I did interview a friend of both Karen and David Swift, a woman named Tonda Brand. She is an educator with the Walnut Ridge School District and knew them both for many years. Tonda and Karen were friends in high school. A few years after high school she was in a college painting class when David approached her. His eyes were beaming. He told Tonda he and Karen had started dating.

"I could tell how proud he was to be with Karen," she said.

Tonda described David as a "good guy." She didn't think there was any way he could have been involved in the murder. She said Karen was a "good girl, with a sweet, mischievous smile." When I did the story with Tonda, I took some flack from some of the slain woman's friends. Several contacted me and told me that Tonda and Karen were not that close, and she had closer friends that knew her better.

I told them it might be true, but I was friends with Tonda and knew her well. She played basketball with Karen and graduated from high school with her. She knew David, and that was enough of a connection for me. I don't understand why this would upset anybody, but it did.

News in the case did break in 2013. In early July, police searched David Swift's home. During the search, he left the house. Investigators spent about three hours at the home, and whatever they found or whatever they were looking for was not disclosed. Box remained tight-lipped. I called David Swift, but he didn't return my phone calls. Police said they had a person of interest in the case by this point, but didn't publicly name the person, to my knowledge.

Police soon turned cold on David Swift. He hired attorney David Farese, a high-powered defense lawyer. He stopped talking to police. But, several months later, he did talk to me.

Persistence is a key tool in a journalist's toolbox, and I just kept calling him. At some point, I knew he couldn't keep putting me off. Finally, we talked. Before the interview began, he said there were several subjects, such as specifics in the case, that he'd been advised by his attorney not to discuss. I told him I understood.

He started by telling me he still had deep feelings for his dead wife, even though they were about to divorce for a second time.

"I love my wife. I love my family. I've been in full cooperation with the police," he said. "No one wants justice more than me."

I asked him why he wasn't talking to the police anymore, according the Dyer County Sheriff's Department. Swift said he had talked exhaustively with investigators and told them everything he knew. He let them search his house and talk to his daughter.

David said he and Karen spoke several times that night, and they didn't get into a fight. Before she drove away, the mother of four drafted a note and left it. The contents of the note were not released. David collected volumes of evidence in the case and was in contact with several private investigators who wanted to help, he said. There were personal details he wanted to talk about, but attorneys advised him to stay silent, he said.

He and Karen had both made mistakes, but he didn't specify what mistakes were made. He said she had a "deeply troubled side" few knew about. He told me he wanted her murder solved, but he didn't want to speculate as to who did it or why. David acknowledged there is a perception by several he is culpable in her death.

Karen's mother, Carol Johnson, told television station WMC Action News 5 in Memphis she thinks David was involved in the homicide. She told the television station the couple was not happy together. David Swift told me he understands why some believe he had some part in the murder, but he didn't do it.

"I know my innocence … God knows my innocence," he said.

I haven't spoken to him since. I am told he moved his family to Blytheville, a town in the far northeast corner of Arkansas. The district attorney's office said, in one of the rare phone calls they returned, the evidence in the case would be presented before a grand jury before any charges are filed.

This case is a true mystery to me. No suspects have been named and the evidence that has been released is scant. My suspicion is the police have little or no real evidence as to what happened to Karen. Her body was in such poor condition when it was found there was probably little or no usable evidence recovered.

Investigators want to speak to David Swift again, but he won't talk to them. That is not suspicious to me. He's following the advice of his attorney. He was the last known person to talk with her, but to this point, nothing has been released by authorities indicating his guilt. In the absence of evidence, I can't make assumptions, so I won't.

I have no real idea who killed her.

As the years pass, and memories fade, I think about the beautiful mother that used to roam the softball and baseball fields in Pocahontas. I've thought a lot about the two sons she left behind, and the two daughters she still needed to raise. There's got to be some evidence, some clue that someone has that will break this case open.

It's solvable, and I hope those children, her grieving mother, and all the other family and friends of Karen Johnson Swift are able to find closure and peace someday.

Henry Greenbaum

"Extinction is the rule. Survival is the exception.

– Carl Sagan

Faige searched desperately in the dark to find her brother, Henry.

She was the only one who could save him. Faige and a Jewish police officer crept in silence. Henry lay perched in the dark. Faige reached out her hand and grasped his. No one uttered a word. The two siblings and the police officer ran. A hole was supposed to be cut in the mangled, barbed wire fence surrounding the labor camp.

Floodlights high above were dark. War insurgents outside the camp promised to cut power lines into the camp, rendering the lights useless. As they made their way to the fence, the lights remained off.

Suddenly, floodlights showered them, a mere 10 feet from the fence.

A hail of bullets descended on Henry, Faige, and their companion. The power hadn't been cut. An impending air raid that night forced the Nazi's to keep the lights off. Dogs barked and men yelled.

One projectile clipped the side of Henry's head and he fell to the ground. Blood poured from the wound. Henry lost sight of Faige and the police officer in the gunfire. He passed out. When he came to, a moment's quick action would mean the difference between life and death.

If guards found him bloody and wounded he would be executed.

Henry gathered himself and ran to a nearby female barracks. He begged them to let him come in. They refused, fearful that harboring him would mean certain death. Eventually, they acquiesced and the 15-year-old was let inside. The women and girls placed rags on his bloody head.

Shouts and bullet fire continued outside. When it subsided, Henry cautiously made his way out of the barracks. Walking through the dark, Henry still heard sporadic shots and guards yelling. As he walked back to his barracks, he caught a glimpse of the hole in the fence.

The police officer lay just on the other side of the fence. Near him was a beautiful clump of blonde hair. Faige was dead. She was the fifth sister he'd seen put to death.

It was 1943, and Henry's horrors were not over.

I don't know what kind of life Henry Greenbaum lived before or after he was subjected to inhumane torture. I don't know what kind of person he is. All I know is that he is one of the most dignified men I've ever encountered.

Each year I speak to journalism students at different colleges and universities. One piece of advice I always give them is to interview people now that you may not get the chance to interview later. World War II veterans and Holocaust survivors, as of this writing, fall into that category.

At least once a year Black River Technical College in Pocahontas, Ark., hosts a Holocaust survivor. Thousands attend these talks, and the speeches given by these individuals are always epic. I make time to cover these events. No one told a more gripping story than Henry Greenbaum.

I first caught a glimpse of him on stage. He was a tall, slender man in his early 80s. He was dressed in a suit. He looked like a college professor preparing to lecture students in a college classroom.

I always tried to make my way up to the stage before the presentations to introduce myself. Henry had a rich, thick accent. I said hello, and just as I did, several others came onto the stage. I am not sure what prompted him to do it, but he rolled up his sleeve exposing a tattoo on his forearm.

It was a serial number, tattooed on him by his Nazi captors. All at once, he went from being a professor to a victim. The stage seemed much darker. He seemed much older. The world became a little colder.

More than once, I've visited the United States Holocaust Memorial Museum in Washington D.C. The displays are thought provoking. The videos are unbelievable. One showed Nazi scientists filling a disabled man's head with air pressure. His eyes danced back and forth, as his cranium swelled. His lips parted, and death met him.

I remember walking through a display with the actual shoes worn by those who were exterminated. I can still smell their odor in the air.

However, nothing was more shocking than the numbers imbedded on Henry's arm. The Holocaust was real for the first time.

I went back to my seat. The tale began.

Henry was born April 1, 1928, in Starachowice, Poland. His father was a tailor by trade and ran a shop inside their home. Henry was one of nine children in the family raised by his mother, Gittel.

His childhood was typical and rather uneventful. Henry attended school, church, and participated in sports. The gangly boy's favorite sport was soccer. Little did he know dark clouds loomed in the west. Poland's powerful European neighbor, Germany, came under Nazi control in 1933. Soon after, Adolph Hitler enacted a number of measures meant to stifle the Jewish population.

Germany also began a campaign to expand her borders. War seemed likely, and Poland was a prime target.

As the calendar flipped to 1939, Nuchem realized his family was in grave danger. In an attempt to spare their lives should the Germans invade Poland, Nuchem sent his son and daughters to work at a munitions factory. Some in the Jewish community believed factory workers might be protected.

Nuchem suddenly died just before Germany invaded Poland on Sept. 1, 1939. Henry, along with his mother, five sisters, and a brother, David, escaped to a farm. Panic gripped the countryside as German soldiers moved towards Poland's capital, Warsaw. The Soviet Union declared war on Poland days later, and Russian troops invaded from the east.

One day while picking tomatoes, David left with a Polish soldier to fight.

By 1940, the Greenbaum family was forced to live in the Starachowice ghetto. The family worked in a factory. Conditions in the ghetto were miserable, Henry said. Food was scarce, families had to live in tight quarters, and the German soldiers and their minions continuously harassed them.

The situation went from bad to tragic.

Henry didn't remember the exact day, but soldiers came into the ghetto and separated his family. Henry and his three sisters who worked in the factory were placed in one line. His mother and two other sisters, who both had children and could not work were placed in a separate line.

Pregnant women, the elderly, young children, and Henry's own nieces and nephews were placed in the same line with his mother. He watched as part of his family was ushered away to the nearby Treblinka Extermination Camp. Henry never saw them again.

"They only left the people who could work ... Treblinka was nothing but a killing center," he said to the crowd.

Silence enveloped the college auditorium as he uttered those words.

Henry's work at the factory was never ending. Workers spent more than 12 hours a day, seven days a week, making all sorts of springs. His sisters, Faige, Chaja, and Yita, were put to work in a tailor shop, sewing Nazi uniforms. He and his sisters were constantly exposed to torture and treatment at the hands of the Nazi soldiers.

The family now resided in a forced labor camp.

The barracks were cruel and miserable. Breakfast consisted of a single slice of moldy bread and a liquid drink that was supposed to be coffee. At night, they got a little cabbage soup, he said. Laborers slept on wooden planks that resembled shelves.

There were no mattresses, or pillows, just a thin blanket. Men and women huddled together in their separate barracks to keep from freezing at night. Lice rampaged the camp and

Henry could not remember ever removing his clothes to take a shower or bath. Conditions were abhorrent and diseases, such as typhoid, consumed the camp, he said.

Many considered death a blessing.

Henry's sister, Chaja, contracted typhoid. She suffered from a high fever and was taken to a camp "hospital," but there was no medicine or doctor to treat her. Chaja was placed on a wooden bed without a mattress or straw to sleep on.

He felt sorry for his dying sister, and he tried to make her life a little more bearable even if it meant a severe beating or death for him. Henry stole clean rags out of the factory each day, and soon he had enough to cobble together a makeshift mattress. Henry snuck his creation into the hospital.

Chaja seemed to do better once the mattress was in place. But one day he went to visit his sister and she wasn't there. He was told the girl died in her sleep.

"It was better for her to go that way," Henry told the silent crowd.

Life continued in the labor camp for Yita, Faige, and Henry, but not for long. Factory shifts were divided into day and night. Henry mostly worked at night. One morning after his shift ended, Henry was headed to his barracks when he noticed a line of people on the other side of a wire fence.

Yita was in line.

Henry ran to the fence and yelled for her.

"I said goodbye," the proud man's voice cracking with emotion. He grabbed his forehead and was visibly distraught.

He doesn't know how Yita died for sure. He never saw her again.

After her death, Faige and others in camp hatched an escape plan. Insurgents outside the camp were supposed to aid their efforts. The day before the planned escape, Faige told her brother. She told him to stay silent and wait for her at the appointed place after dark.

The image of the blonde hair burned deep, but it wasn't until the next morning that Henry learned for sure his sister was no more. When she did not answer at the morning roll call, he knew she was dead.

Once the escape attempt failed, Henry returned to his toil in the spring factory. He was now 15 years old and nearly every person he'd known as a child was now dead. His father. His mother. His sisters. Even the nieces and nephews he had hardly known.

A torture room was set up in the factory and twice Henry was taken there. The teenager was repeatedly lashed with a whip. His cries and begs for mercy were met with more lashes.

He warned the students they never wanted to be brutalized in that manner.

Henry's struggle was about to get worse. By 1944, the German armies were being routed on all fronts. Slave laborers were shifted from camp to camp to avoid the garrisons of foreign soldiers who now encroached on the Third Reich's new European empire. The Polish teen was shipped to Auschwitz, the most infamous concentration camp operated by the Nazis.

The train ride there was written out of a horror movie. More than 100 people were shoved into a car that could maybe hold a third that number. Passengers went days on end without food or water.

Passengers savagely fought each other over premium spots in the car to catch a whiff of fresh air. People began to die. Rotting corpses littered the floor. The stench, even for hardened slave camp laborer like Henry Greenbaum was intolerable.

Once the train ride ended, chaos erupted. Workers were herded into separate lines. One meant life, the other death. Henry said he was too starved and weak to care. He once again was chosen to live. His reward for the next three months was perhaps the most disturbing jobs he did during the entire war.

"I stacked rotted corpses," he said. The stiff, mangled bodies were like firewood, he said. Day after day, he moved dead bodies while a thin veil of ash floated in the air. The crematories were working in full force, burning the bodies of the dead. However, they could not keep up, he said. Ashes flowed out of the crematories like snowflakes."

A German businessman chose Henry to work in a satellite camp, one owned by the I.G. Farben Company. The company made munitions, synthetic rubber, and fuel. Henry helped construct a road to the factory.

Hunger was a constant in the camp. One of Henry's roommates left their barracks and crept into the night. He brought back a pile of garbage. They ate it, Henry said.

"When you're hungry, you'll eat just about anything," he told the students.

The roommate escaped again, but this time he was caught. Nazi guards hung him for stealing garbage that he planned to eat.

Day and night, Henry and his companions heard bombs exploding in the distance. Allied bombers were hitting targets closer and closer to them. Occasionally, the workers would come across British prisoners of war. The prisoners told them the war would end soon.

Bombing raids forced the Germans to move the slave labor camp. Henry was relocated to the Flossenburg Concentration Camp, along the Czechoslovakian border. American bombers harassed the train on its way to the camp, Henry said.

Bombs pounded the tracks. The German soldiers "scattered like rats" each time the bombings began. Henry and the other slave laborers took much glee in this, he said. Nobody cared if a bomb hit the train and killed them. It was worth it to see their captors suffering, he said.

His stay at the camp was brief. The Russian army lurked in the east and the bombing raids became more intense. Each day Henry began to hold out hope that he would be free. One morning he stepped outside and what he saw he couldn't believe.

Soccer goals were being erected. A contingent from the Red Cross was set to visit the camp. The German soldiers wanted it to look like the prisoners had the opportunity to play games when they weren't toiling.

Henry was stunned. He loved soccer and missed it dearly. However, no one had the energy or wanted to kick a ball, he said. To further the ruse, the soldiers brought the workers bowls of cream of wheat to eat that night, instead of the standard cabbage water meal.

When the Red Cross team left, the soccer goals were removed and there was no more cream of wheat. It was back to water and cabbage, he said.

Brutal winter conditions hit central Europe in February 1945. Continued Allied raids forced the Germans to move the camp once more. Perhaps the most arduous moment during his entire enslavement was about to begin. The rail lines had been obliterated and the Germans decided to move their slave workers to the Dachau Concentration Camp in southern Germany, not far from the Austrian border.

For three months, the workers stammered in the bitter cold. The meager food rations were gone. Each day people died in the muck, he said. Henry spent three months on a death march to Dachau. At night, they slept on the cold ground.

If they happened upon a farm, the soldiers might let them eat a raw potato, but that was rare, Henry said. One night they slept in a straw-filled silo. He said it was like sleeping in a fancy hotel to them. They not only slept on the straw; They chewed it up and swallowed it, too, he said.

Henry's ordeal came to a sudden and terrifying end April 24, 1945. The laborers were on a farm when a low-flying plane suddenly appeared in the sky. The soldiers ushered them into some nearby woods. Henry thought the soldiers might shoot them.

One way or another, his suffering was about to end.

After they walked for two hours, the soldiers grabbed their guard dogs and left. Henry and his companions were puzzled. At first, they thought it might be a sick trick, and the soldiers were hiding in the woods, tempting them to run for it. Henry thought if he tried to leave, he might be met with bullets.

The slave workers decided to leave. They came upon a highway and a tank rumbled towards them. The hatch opened and an American soldier smiled at them and told them the war was over.

"He said we were liberated," Henry said.

The American soldiers gave the starving group their food rations. Henry and the others were taken to a farm. He was told a feast was being prepared. When they got to the house, he and the other workers saw buckets of potato peelings in the yard.

He grabbed a bucket and started eating. In his starve crazed mind, the peelings were a feast, he said. When they walked inside food was prepared, but they were too full to eat.

Henry's life soon became a whirlwind. He set out to find any relatives who might have survived. Two brothers, David and Zachary, survived the Holocaust. They, along with Henry, moved to the United States following the war. There they joined their sister, Dina, who moved to the U.S. in 1937.

Eventually, Henry married a woman named Shirley, and the couple raised four children. Henry said he does not know how or why he survived when so many died around him. An unfettered belief in God guided the man throughout his struggle, he said.

The students gave Henry a thunderous ovation at the end of his speech. After his talk, students clamored to have pictures taken with him.

Before the cameras started to clack, I got one more chance to talk with Henry. I asked him how often he thinks about his internment and the family members he lost. Tears welled in the old man's aged face and his forehead wrinkled.

He put his hand on his face to cover his mouth. The remorse nearly overwhelmed him. I hated myself for asking the question. Even after all these years, his pain was deep, and palpable. In a stoic moment, he quickly wiped away the tears and spoke with two strong words.

I will never forget his response, spoken by a truly remarkable man.

"Every day."

Estelle Laughlin

"I shall never forget the little faces of the children, whose bodies turned into wreaths of smoke beneath a silent, blue sky."

– Elie Wiesel, Holocaust survivor

Dolls littered the ground and red streams flowed. Estelle Laughlin tried not to look. The images seemed unreal, and too terrible to comprehend. She walked faster, averting her eyes from the truth.

The faces looked as if they were fired from clay. Men and women. Boys and girls. Most were dressed in ragged, filthy garments. A few looked familiar.

They were faces, but they were not made of clay. They were made of human flesh. Makeshift streams filled with blood covered the streets. It was 1943 and Estelle, a Polish Jew, was being escorted out of the Warsaw ghetto by Nazi soldiers.

Estelle witnessed plenty of death and blood while encamped in the ghetto. However, this was different. Many of the mangled and dead were her family and friends. Their lives forever lost in the slaughter. When she did catch a glimpse, the bodies, and especially the faces, did not look real.

Her father, Samek, had been part of resistance effort inside the ghetto. After a fierce firefight, the Nazis prevailed. Samek and his family were now headed to the dreaded Majdanek Concentration Camp.

The family was about to experience even more agony and horror.

She came to Northeast Arkansas in October 2009 to share her tale at Black River Technical College in Pocahontas. Thousands of students came to listen to her. She is one of the few children who survived the Warsaw ghetto. It's estimated that less than 1% of youths, under the age of 14 who entered the Warsaw ghetto, survived the war. Estelle made it out alive, but the cost was overwhelming.

Quiet and unassuming, the elderly woman was dressed immaculately the first time I saw her. A soft glow encompassed her. She had kind eyes.

Hundreds of students squirmed anxiously in their seats before she spoke. Following my own custom, I approached her before her talk. She had a soft voice with a thick Polish accent. Goodness radiated from this woman and it was hard to imagine the pain and suffering she had endured.

We chatted for a few minutes and then she took the stage.

Her life began typically. Estelle was born July 9, 1929, in Warsaw. She and her older sister, Freda, attended a local school and her father worked as a jeweler. Their simple world changed Sept. 1, 1939.

German army columns invaded Poland. The Nazi's had invented a new type of war, called Blitzkrieg or lightening war. For hundreds of years armies in Europe fought slow, methodical battles mostly on traditional battlefields. Blitzkrieg was different.

The Germans employed fast moving Panzer tank divisions. Before they swept into a country, the German Air Force, or Luftwaffe, would swoop in and decimate the area with bombs and missiles. The shock an awe of the German's modern military equipment and tactics left the Polish Army reeling.

A second fatal blow came just weeks into the invasion. German leader Adolf Hitler made a secret pact with the Soviet Union and its dictator, Joseph Stalin. The two leaders decided to divide Poland. Days later, Soviet Union forces invaded from the east and Poland was no more.

Estelle and her sister were not allowed to attend school after the Germans took control in Warsaw. There were 400,000 Jews living in the city at the time. They had to wear patches shaped like the Star of David, a Jewish symbol. By 1940, all Jews in the city were forced to live in a ghetto. The ghetto was 1.3 square miles in size.

Families were forced to live together in cramped apartments.

Food was scarce. The meager rations were not enough to sustain the population in the ghetto. Samek was able to buy extra food on the black market to keep his wife and daughters alive. Anyone who owned a book could be sentenced to death. Teaching was forbidden.

Not long after the ghetto was established, Jews were transferred to Treblinka II, an extermination camp. Soldiers came into the ghetto and took people away. Virtually none returned.

Estelle and her family survived by hiding in a secret room where the Germans could not find them. She and her sister were able to get some schooling during this time, and the family even arranged for them to see live plays at a Christian church.

In July 1942, the ghetto was liquidated for the first time. Soldiers stormed the streets killing innocent people and stealing others away. Estelle hid in a secret compartment behind her family's wardrobe closet. Nazi soldiers entered the room.

Each clack of their boots was like a gunshot piercing her heart, she said.

The soldiers sifted through the closets. They laughed and told jokes. Outside on the streets murderous screams and gunfire filled the air. Behind the closet, Estelle waited anxiously. If they found her, she would die on the spot. The soldiers did not seem human; they were more like animals, she said.

"You can't imagine the pounding of those boots," she said.

One of Estelle's friends, Lucia, had a dog. It barked and growled at the soldiers. They didn't kill it. Instead, they followed the animal. It led them into an apartment and to a bed. Between the box spring and the mattress, Lucia hid.

"And that was the end of her," Estelle said with sorrow in her voice.

Estelle wasn't discovered. That night, her father read Yiddish books to them using a carbide light to illuminate the darkness. The light created an orb around them. Estelle said her father's words and the surrounding light made her feel safe even though soldiers still roamed the ghetto.

Her miserable life continued.

By 1943, most of the Jews in the ghetto had been slaughtered or moved to slave labor camps. Several who remained decided to form a resistance force, and Samek was among them.

Samek and his comrades found inventive ways to secure arms. They would wade through the dingy Warsaw sewer system to the Christian section of the city. They were able to acquire arms and they prepared to fight the SS who regularly patrolled their neighborhoods, she said.

Tensions rose further when the SS ordered all Jewish orphans out of the ghetto to be killed in the gas chamber. Dr. Janusz Korczak ran the ghetto orphanage. Korczak was a famous doctor whose talents were well known throughout Europe. A Christian resistance group decided to liberate him.

However, he refused.

Korczak didn't want his orphans to die alone. The good doctor led his band of orphans out of the ghetto and into certain death. Before they left he handed each one a little Jewish flag. He was like a father to them and he could not let them go, Estelle said.

A firefight broke out in April when the SS and other police units moved in. The Germans decided to liquidate the 55,000 or so Jews who were left into slave labor camps. The resistance forces fought back. Samek placed his family in a makeshift bunker in the basement of a house.

Estelle said her father was a dignified, kind man who deeply loved his family. He was also courageous and wanted his home liberated.

Fierce fights broke out in the ghetto. Artillery shells met the police. Estelle, her mother, and sister stayed in the bunker. A ticking clock let them know if it was night or day.

A French tutor who shared the bunker gave them lessons to help pass the time. Another carbide light helped illuminate the dark bunker.

The Nazis retaliated by razing the ghetto brick by brick. A bomb blew apart the house, exposing the bunker. The resistance was over. Samek and his family were headed to a concentration camp.

There was little doubt Samek would meet his death there. Surprisingly, his family was allowed to live. When they arrived, he was placed in a line headed to the gas chamber, while his wife and daughters were placed in a separate line.

Estelle couldn't take it.

Her beloved father was moments from death. She broke rank and rushed to his line. Samek begged his daughter to return before the soldiers saw her. The teenage girl smiled at her father and opened her coat. Inside was a vial of cyanide. Jews carried poison with them as an alternative to whatever manner of death the Nazi's decided to bestow on them at a moments notice.

Samek calmed down, and looked into his daughter's eyes one last time.

"Oh, no," he said. "You must live."

It crushed Estelle, but she obeyed her father's last command. She left him in line and went back to her mother. Moments later, her beloved father was gone. Ashes of the dead lingered in the air.

Living conditions in the labor camp were unbearable. Lice infested the camp and Estelle suffered from severe bruises, a byproduct of tortuous, forced labor. Bloody scabs oozed constantly. She and her mother cut turf. There was no point to the work, but it occupied their time, she said.

At night, they would eat turnip soup and bread scraps.

Once they were given soap to take a shower. Many Jews knew what that meant. They weren't going to get clean. They were about to be gassed.

However, the Nazi's overestimated how many Jews they could kill at a time and the Warsaw ghetto liquidation left them overcrowded, she said. So they actually got to take a shower, the first one they had taken in months.

A soldier beat Freda so badly she couldn't work. Estelle and her mother tried to hide Freda in the barracks, but eventually she was caught. Freda's name was placed on a list. Estelle thought it was a gas chamber list. She and her mother opted to join Freda. They swapped identities with other refugees. Estelle and her family were weary and had no will to live any longer, she said.

"We wanted to die together, as a family."

The move saved their lives.

Estelle, Michla, and Freda were moved to the Skarzysko Concentration Camp. The women toiled for months in a munitions factory. They were moved to another munitions factory before they were liberated in 1945. Her first meal after she was freed was a dill pickle.

The family moved to Bavaria to escape the Soviet occupation. In 1947, they moved to New York City.

Throughout her ordeal in the camps, Estelle and her friends wrote poetry and stories about their incarceration. The tales described the joy they had before the war and the camps.

Estelle said she still carries those words in her heart to this day.

She never carried a grudge. Her father would not want it that way.

"I wondered sometimes what does death feel like? But then I remembered the face of humanity. I remembered the nobility of humanity."

The curious case of Rebekah Gould

"Any man's death diminishes me because I am involved in mankind; And therefore never send to know for whom the bell tolls; It tolls for thee."

- John Donne

Rebekah's story.

Sisters Danielle and Rebekah Gould had a long journey in front of them. They had recently moved to Fayetteville, Ark., to attend college. Rebekah was 22 at the time and Danielle was a year younger. The two rode together and headed for their hometown of Mountain View.

They sang and laughed as the road twisted and turned towards their former home. At one point, they had a flat tire, and in typical fashion, Rebekah decided to change it herself. The 5'2' girl that weighed about 100 pounds was up to the task, and the journey continued. At another point during the trip, which began on or about Sept. 17, 2004, Rebekah received a text message from a former love interest, Casey McCullough. He was a little younger than she was, and the two had dated off and on for about a year. The former couple worked together at a local Sonic, in the town of Melbourne.

McCullough lived in a trailer house on a piece of family property near the town of Guion, in rural Izard County. It is an isolated spot. The message made Rebekah roll her eyes, Danielle said years later. She had no intention of reigniting the relationship, but she planned to stay at his house that weekend, the sister said.

"It's Casey ... he wants to be exclusive," she said to her sister.

It was clear to Danielle that Rebekah did not intend to date him anymore, but lingering relationships at this age are difficult for many to navigate. Danielle wasn't the only person who knew about her sister's future intentions. Weeks before, she spoke to her dad, Dr. Larry Gould. She told him she was moving on with her life, and there was no place for McCullough in it.

The road finally ended in Mountain View. It was time for the sisters, who had been companions since Danielle's birth to say goodbye. She was slated to spend time with her boyfriend, Nick, that weekend. Rebekah was notorious for not having minutes on the cheap, Nokia phone she used. The sisters planned to return to Fayetteville on Monday, Sept. 20, 2004. Rebekah was supposed to pick Danielle up at their mother's house at noon.

When the sisters parted that day, they would never speak again. Rebekah drove off into the distance.

Noon that Monday came and went. Rebekah never arrived. She never called. Danielle and her mother flew into a panic. They repeatedly called McCullough, a guy who had been Danielle's friend, too, according to her. As the afternoon turned into early evening, as the summer solstice prepared to turn into the fall equinox, it became clear.

Rebekah Gould was missing. As the world turned from summer to fall, the beautiful college student was turning from life into death.

It's been more than 14 years, and her mysterious murder still haunts the hills and the hamlets in this part of the Ozark Mountains. The police have never even been able to publicly name an official suspect in the case, but McCullough has always been a person of interest, according to the Arkansas State Police. The case has been bizarre, and at times mind blowing. A conclusion is desperately sought.

I had been a journalist and author for only a few months when Rebekah vanished. It was the first murder case I'd ever covered as a journalist. I have written many news stories through the years, and included a chapter about the case in my true crime books, *Witches in West Memphis,* and *The Creek Side Bones*. Not a lot of new information filtered out about the unsolved, cold case until I received and email from Catherine Townsend, a reporter with the Discovery Channel in March 2018. I had never heard of her until that point. In the email, she asked to meet with me. Her intention was to put together a podcast, *Hell and Gone*. It would feature Rebekah's case.

Little did I know at the time it would turn into a potential game changer. I agreed to meet with Catherine and her team. We met in a coffee shop in the little town of Hardy, about an hour from Melbourne. We spent hours talking, and I began with a brief history of my involvement in the case. The team began to record. I began to talk.

I was sitting at my desk inside the Areawide Media office, in Salem, Ark., on Sept. 22, 2004, when the phone rang. It was Wednesday, the slowest day of the week for me. Our newspaper was a weekly, and our deadline was Tuesday. On Wednesdays, I typically took newspapers to the city halls and courthouses that were on my beat. I received the call mid-morning, around 9 or 10, and usually I would have been gone by then. The person on the line told me there was a missing college student in Melbourne.

Excited, I ran out the door. I had been waiting for a big scoop as a new reporter and this might be it. I didn't know it then, but no story would cause me more anguish.

When I arrived at the Izard County Sheriff's Department, I was angry, however. She had been missing for two days and the Izard County Sheriff Joe Martz didn't mention there was a missing college student when I spoke to him the day before – a tremendous omission, and an irresponsible one. Media coverage helps in missing cases. It doesn't hurt. I confronted Martz in the parking lot. I always liked him, but I had a job to do.

He gave me a line about not wanting to compromise the integrity of the investigation. I dealt with him for a few moments, but my focus quickly turned to the family. Her mother, Shirley Ballard, handed me a missing poster with a description of the missing woman.

She spent the weekend with McCullough. She dropped him off at work at 8 a.m. on Sept. 20, 2004, the same Monday she went missing. After dropping him off, she stopped at a local convenience store and bought a breakfast biscuit and some other items. She went back to McCullough's house.

At some point that morning, she vanished. McCullough claims he was at work all day, and afterwards went to Batesville with a group of friends to pick up his truck, eat dinner, and watch a movie. He said he never went home that day or night. Two friends, Phillip and Larron confirmed he was with them all night.

In sworn statements to police, the two friends said they were "shocked" that he wanted to hang out with them. He rarely visited with friends, and spent most of his time with Rebekah, they both said. Few of his friends had been to his house. During the night, McCullough borrowed Larron's phone and made a few calls. He told the two friends that Rebekah was missing. Larron and Phillip, in these sworn statements taken days after she disappeared, both said they were surprised that he didn't leave to try to find her.

Danielle told me she spent that night calling McCullough's cell phone repeatedly.

"He wouldn't answer his damn phone … I couldn't understand that," she said. "To this day I don't understand it."

Why he didn't go home to get a fresh set of clothes after work remains a mystery. He stayed the night at Larron's house. The next morning he left the house around 7 a.m. to go to work. He returned to his home that morning at one point and there were damning signs. Rebekah's car was there as was her dog, Lady. Her purse, money, keys, clothes, and other personal items were there, too. McCullough noticed that his mattress had been flipped and the sheets were missing. He left his house and went to work, according to him.

This is where his account of what happened that morning differs from the police. By 8:30 a.m., the Izard County Sheriff's Department had been notified by Rebekah's family that she was missing. McCullough told me during an interview in 2005 he found out at work that she was missing and that he left work to go and try to find her. On his way back to his house, he encountered a police officer, Charlie Melton, and he led Melton back to his locked house.

I thought the story was a little strange. McCullough lived a short distance from the Sonic, and didn't know Melton. I wondered, even then, how he just happened upon the police officer. When I interviewed him at that time and again in 2006, I didn't know that he told family and friends he'd gone to the trailer prior to when he went with police. I also didn't know he'd told his friends the previous night she was missing.

So, at the very least, he lied to me.

Melton told the *Batesville Guard* in 2008 he received a call to do a wellness check at McCullough's house and went to the Sonic to talk with him. The two then left the Sonic together and went to his house. This story made more sense to me. When the doors were opened, pets, including Lady had "messed" in the house according to Melton. The officer used the words dogs and pets to describe what was in the house. Rebekah's stuff was still there including the uneaten breakfast sandwich.

On the back porch, which was surrounded by a fence with a gate, Melton found traces of blood. In the washing machine, bloody sheets were found and blood was in the washing machine's agitator. Blood was splattered on the walls and baseboards in different parts of the house. The killer went to "great pains" to clean the house, Melton said.

McCullough looked shocked when the blood was discovered, Melton said. Investigators spent 12 hours bagging evidence from inside the home. The search began.

The next day, Sept. 22, 2004, is the day I arrived at the Sheriff's Department. Danielle was out searching for her sister when she came across a potential piece of evidence. Police told searchers to be on the lookout for a coffee cup.

Rebekah's coffee cup wasn't recovered during the evidence sweep of the house. Danielle found one on a gravel road, but it turned out to not be the right one. The coffee cup was eventually found days later – inside the microwave at McCullough's house.

The fact that she disappeared from his house and he was a love interest made McCullough a natural suspect, even according to him. The first time I saw him officers were escorting him into the Sheriff's Department. He was interviewed for many hours and took three polygraphs. He claims he passed all three, but I'm curious why they would have ordered the third one if he cleared the first two.

He claimed to have been at work, and there are rumors a video shows him at work all day. I am told that's not true. Danielle contacted one of the former owners at the Sonic and he told her video surveillance system there at the time recycled over itself, and the police missed getting the video by a day. That would make sense since he hasn't been officially cleared, according to ASP.

The next days merged together. I watched Larry, Shirley, the sisters, and others search the fields and hills in and around Guion. I will never forget watching Larry tape a missing poster to a guilde arrow sign on a steep curve. It became clear Rebekah would not be found alive. One person I never saw searching for Rebekah was Casey McCullough or anyone from his family. Family members later claimed that there had been threats made against him, but I thought that was odd because Rebekah only had sisters and a father who at that time was pushing 60 years old.

A few days passed and Monday morning arrived. My body pulsed with energy and I drove to Melbourne. I overheard a few ladies talking at the courthouse. Apparently, searchers where concentrating on a stretch of Arkansas 9, a road that connects Melbourne with the town of Mountain View. I was told that Sheriff Martz had a hunch it might be the right place to look. A lot has been made of that "hunch" in the media and social media through the years.

It was no hunch. A woman called the police and told them there was an odd smell in the vicinity where she was found and vultures flew overhead. Investigators wanted to protect the identity of the caller and never revealed why they chose to search in that spot.

I drove down the highway and noticed vultures swirling in the sky. The day was sunny and bright. A few miles passed the Sheriff's Department, I came upon a series of vehicles along the highway. I parked my truck and got out. It was in this moment I encountered Rebekah Gould for the first and only time.

In my first book, *Witches in West Memphis* I said that she had been covered by a tarp, which at some point I assume she was to preserve evidence at the scene. I did not describe her because I did not want to bring pain to the family, and I did not want to interfere with the police investigation. Many details had still not been released to the public. I included a description in my second book *The Creek Side Bones* after I learned the family had a copy of her autopsy report, and Larry had read it.

That was a mistake on my part. When Danielle read my description of her sister in that book, she said it caused her a lot of anguish. I felt horrible when she told me that.

Rebekah was found laying on the ground in a sleeveless t-shirt and panties. The shirt had the word "music" on it. The man, who found her, Lee Arnold, told me he could see her belly-button ring. She was found about 35 feet from the highway among a scattering of tree limbs, bushes, and other foliage. What Arnold saw that day haunted him for many years afterwards, he told me.

Arnold said he found her body a few minutes into the search. He, along with two other volunteers were directed to search in that area that morning, he said. Her body was reportedly found just a few miles from Larron's then house, and there is a little used road, Lunenberg Road that connects Arkansas 9 with Arkansas 58 near McCullough's house. It didn't take the killer long to transport her body from the house to this spot.

Her skull was partially skeletonized on the left side. She died from one or two blows, according to her official autopsy report and an independent analysis Larry had done once the report was released. Pieces of facial bone were never recovered. Her soft tissues, including her eyes and brain were gone. There were no defensive wounds to her body, according to the radiological report. Nothing was discovered under her fingernails, per the autopsy.

Rebekah still had her panties on and there were no signs she had been sexually assaulted, according to the report. Decomposition in that part of her body was so advanced that it couldn't be determined whether she was sexually assaulted or not, however, the report states. Rebekah was feisty and would have fought someone molesting her, Danielle told me. The autopsy report also states her breasts were in normal condition, with no wounds. No semen or foreign pubic hairs were found in her or on her underwear. There were no other reported injuries to her body, and the fact that she was still wearing her undergarments leads to the logical conclusion she was not sexually assaulted.

The report stated she could have possibly been strangled. There was no evidence of this, but her neck had decomposed to the point that it couldn't be definitively ruled out. The analysis Larry Gould had performed years later came to the same conclusion, but also noted there would be other types of evidence to support that if it happened and there was none. What remained of her neck appeared to be uninjured, according to the report.

The medical examiners and the independent firm hired by Larry to examine the evidence in her case came to the same conclusion. She died from a single or possibly two, lethal blows to the left side of her face.

"Although limited, the autopsy findings indicate that blunt force head injuries were the most likely cause of the death. There is a reasonably good correlation between the observed injuries and the location were the injuries were sustained. Inside the residence where she was staying, there was blood present, along with evidence of a clean-up," the report states.

A short time after the murder, I learned that something else was missing from McCullough's house – a loose piano leg.

It has never been recovered, and a quick examination of the wound pattern to her face indicates it was the murder weapon or an object very similar. Danielle told me months before her sister died McCullough showed them the piano leg and how easily it became dislodged from an old piano he kept inside his house.

I stood on the embankment for only a moment. It was surreal. It was one of the most unforgettable moments of my life. Sheriff Martz directed traffic on the highway. I left and went to the Sheriff's Department. Unbelievable grief met me. People were crying in the parking lot as I pulled in. Larry confronted me. There was a rumor that a body had been found.

He asked me if they'd found her body. I told him he needed to talk to the sheriff. He grabbed me and asked me if they'd found his girl. I couldn't lie to him. I said it's true. He was the father of a murdered woman. He clinched me for a second. Tears stirred in his eyes. Moments later, he charged into the Sheriff's Department to seek answers.

The day lingered. During my wait, I drove down Arkansas 9 a time or two just to fill time. No news was forthcoming. Officials announced there would be a press conference that afternoon.

Lt. Bill Beach with the Arkansas State Police led the presser. He said it was the opinion of the investigators that there was a lot of blood at McCullough's house. He also said that McCullough was not an official suspect at that time.

I left and went back to my office to write my first story about Rebekah Gould. I spent the better part of the night writing, and then re-writing my story. Her missing poster was propped on my desk. I have kept it to this day, and it still has the notes on it that I took when I first encountered her family.

Her funeral was held a few days after her autopsy. Her high school boyfriend, Justin Gullett, served as a pallbearer and short time later would give his newborn daughter Rebekah's name. McCullough's friends and family claim he went to the funeral, but Danielle, an aunt, and Larry Gould all claim they didn't see him there. Danielle said he might have been in the parking lot, but she couldn't remember for sure. Larry sent me pictures of the signatures of the people that signed the guest book. McCullough's close friend, Patrick Goings, signed the book. If Casey went, why can't anyone remember him there, and where is his signature in the book?

I assumed this would be an easy murder to solve. She was killed in the house from a blow to the head and then tossed on the side of the road. It was obviously a crime of passion. Her money was not taken, her car was still there, and the killer didn't even hurt her dog. In fact, the dog, and possibly another pet were unharmed in the house. This was such an odd detail to me. There is no way that animal didn't follow the killer when he dragged her body to that back porch.

What killer would put the dog or dogs back in the house? Wouldn't the killer, if unknown to the animals, be attacked by the dogs and been injured?

Days turned to weeks, and then months, and before I knew it years. I moved to other newspapers and other murder cases. Every so often, I wrote or read a Rebekah Gould story. For some reason, her case remained unsolved.

By 2016, I'd written my first true crime book and included a chapter about her case. I wanted to include it to raise awareness and hopefully get it solved. I was at a book signing one day pitching my book to a friendly man. My first book was primarily about the West Memphis Three, the infamous case in which three teenagers – Damien Echols, Jason Baldwin, and Jessie Misskelley Jr. – were wrongfully convicted of the deaths of three 8-year-old boys in West Memphis, Ark., in 1993.

Numerous documentaries, books, and even a Hollywood movie has been made about the internationally famous case. I had interviewed Echols while he still sat on Arkansas' Death Row and had written more news stories about that case than any other journalist in the world. I had interviewed every single person involved on both sides of the case, and it was only natural that I'd write a book about it. However, I wanted to include a chapter about Rebekah, and I told the man to please read about her as I ended the pitch.

I asked him if he wanted to buy a book. He said no. He wanted 10. My friend, A.K. Barnes was taking pictures for a magazine spread about the book as I spoke to the man. I told her "whatever I just told him, I need to tell everybody," as a joke. I flipped the first cover over. I asked the man who I needed to make it out to. He pulled a pink ribbon from his pocket. It had a picture on it.

"I know who you are," I said to him.

He pulled a cross from a bag with Rebekah's picture on it. He told me it was what he kept on his desk. The man was obviously Dr. Larry Gould. We hugged and cried for a bit. He sat with me for a long while and we chatted. Little did I know this would be the beginning of a new odyssey, a new chapter in the Rebekah Gould story.

A few weeks later, I had a book signing at Dr. Gould's office in Mountain Home. The former Lawrence County Sheriff Jody Dotson along with the current Baxter County Sheriff John Montgomery, two men I'd done stories with in the past, stopped by and wished me well. During this signing, something odd happened.

A man showed up and I pitched him the book. Towards the end of the pitch, he identified himself as Arkansas State Police Special Agent Dennis Simmons, the lead detective in the Gould murder probe. He told me he came to the signing to see what I knew about the case. He had driven all the way from Mountain View. My first thought was why he didn't just call me.

We spoke for a moment. He told me he was 90% sure who did it, but getting to the last 10% might be impossible. The implication was clear. This case might not be solved. A little while later, I saw him talking to Larry. After Simmons left, Larry told me the lead investigator told him there was almost no forensic evidence in the case. I guess the amount of evidence could be dependent on who you think committed the crime, however.

Along with A.K., I wrote several stories about her case for several local newspapers that summer. Dr. Gould had received an anonymous letter from someone claiming to have overheard a conversation. We wrote about it, and the case began to heat up once more. That heat soon died, and it went dormant once more. In September of that year, I decided to contact McCullough again to see if he'd learned anything new about the case.

I met with Dr. Gould numerous times during this period and he was convinced that Casey was the primary suspect in the case. I thought the police had cleared him based on powerful alibi evidence. It would have to be powerful. She died in his house, likely on his bed, from a blow delivered with a loose piano leg that belonged to him. The killer tried to clean the house up.

Who would clean-up the mess? Why move the body? What killer would have the gall to use someone else's washing machine?

Being in that house for any length of time would be a major risk, and the killer left her stuff including her car and dog. Each of these actions enhanced the killer's chances of being caught. The only reasonable explanation was that leaving her body and not cleaning up the blood were greater threats in the killer's mind. None of that makes any sense at all. It was during this time I started hearing stories that McCullough did go back to his house before the police did the wellness check. This was a vital detail to me. If he went back to that house that was a major problem for him, in my mind.

I called the Sonic in Melbourne one afternoon to see if anybody had any idea about how to contact him. Unbelievably, his wife was at the Sonic. We spoke for a few minutes on the phone. She was warm and friendly. She said McCullough had read my first book, and liked it. She gave me his cell number and said he would gladly speak with me. She even went the further step of telling me to friend him on Facebook, and message him because cell service was spotty at their house.

After I left about a half a dozen messages during the next few days it became evident he didn't want to speak. I found out he was still living in the same house where Rebekah was slain. I called the Sonic a second time, and his wife was there again. This time she was cold and distant. She said McCullough would now only speak to the police and moments later, she hung up the phone.

I was stunned. During those few days, I had not written anything about the case, and to that point, I was the only person to interview McCullough. I wrote a story with him in 2005, and talked to him again in 2006. To that point, I'd never written a single word that might indicate he had anything to do with the murder. After this, I became suspicious.

In 2017, I released my second true crime book, *The Creek Side Bones*. It also included a chapter about Rebekah's case. I got a lot of social media messages, but no solid leads. Several different podcasters contacted me for interviews, and each time I told their listeners about Rebekah Gould.

When I finished with Catherine Townsend and her crew that day, we stayed in touch. She did two follow-up interviews and as the spring and summer unfolded in 2018, she came across some remarkable evidence.

At least one of McCullough's former co-workers claim he confessed to them. He even signed a sworn affidavit and gave it to investigators. During the *Hell and Gone* podcast, the man, who I've chosen not to identify, said that McCullough told him he dumped her body and threw the piano leg off a bridge into the nearby White River. I know the river was searched more than once. The reason he killed her was that she was ending their relationship. The man making this claim didn't know anybody in Rebekah's family at that time.

Catherine interviewed this man in late spring or early summer 2018. Up to that point, there wasn't a single news story that had that detail. Only a handful of family members, including Larry and Danielle, knew Rebekah planned to end things with him. It didn't become public knowledge until October 2018 when Larry and Catherine appeared on the *Dr. Oz* show to promote the podcast.

How did he know Rebekah planned to end the relationship?

Catherine interviewed many key players in the case, and the sworn statements given by Phillip and Larron were emailed to her. The increased public scrutiny in the case led Simmons to re-interview some of the original witnesses, and Catherine told me he sent the original statements back to Phillip and Larron to "freshen" their memories.

What?

This seemed crazy to me. Why would he send statements back to a witness? There may be a legitimate reason, but I've asked a lot of my friends in law enforcement about this, and none of them could come up with one. In fact, most can't believe a detective would send statements back to witnesses. A detective would want to compare and contrast the statements from then and now, I was told.

When the *Hell and Gone* podcast began in October of 2018, it ignited a firestorm. Catherine methodically tracked down a list of potential suspects and many of them spoke to her on the record. Each week she revealed details in the case, and squashed several what seemed to be bogus theories. I wasn't thrilled with the material she used from me at the beginning of the series, but as it progressed, it got better. It became so popular that it was spoofed on *Saturday Night Live*.

Group pages formed on social media sites and people started taking sides. Several of Rebekah's family members began to attack one another as the series continued. I tried my best to stay out of it, but inevitably, my name was brought into the fold. I will not go into great detail, but it was so strange to me that family members would attack me. I am a journalist and a writer. This is my profession and I've covered lots of murder cases.

I did make one mistake in this case. I let it become personal, especially with my relationships with the family. I typically keep family members at arm's length, but not this time. Accusations swirled around Larry, his daughters and others connected to the case. I was bombarded with social media messages.

The podcast seemed to initially clear McCullough, the last several episodes squarely focused on him. McCullough was the only person who refused to speak to Catherine. She played an audio recording of the co-worker's recollection of McCullough confessing. The co-worker said it happened four separate times, and there were times when he was drunk when he confessed.

At this juncture, I don't know what to think anymore. I think the police believe she died later in the day on Sept. 20, 2004, and I think that maybe hampering their investigation. I have often been asked how well the case has been investigated. There are several troubling aspects of this investigation.

First, officers spent 12 hours in the house and somehow missed her coffee cup in the microwave. Danielle is obviously the person who knew Rebekah the best, including her habits and potential people she might have been dating at the time. Danielle told me she doesn't remember giving the police a formal statement and they have rarely talked to her.

This is important because in the *Hell and Gone* podcast, a man came forward claiming that he dated Rebekah just prior to her murder. He details an incident where he and Rebekah was hanging out at a house and Casey showed up. Casey was very animated and hit a door at one point. Danielle confirmed the story.

Have the police interviewed this other potential love interest?

Rebekah had two couches inside Casey's house. After her death, Danielle took the couches with her to Fayetteville. About two years later, Simmons and another detective went to Danielle's house to collect cushions from the couches to search for possible forensic or DNA evidence.

Two years later?

When the pod cast ended, I thought the story would begin to fade once more. I received an email that dramatically shifted the focus. Easily the most qualified person to ever look at this case was about to appear on the scene. Jennifer Bucholtz, a counter intelligence agent who served tours of duty in Afghanistan and Iraq sent me an email Jan. 30, 2019. She wanted to study Rebekah's case.

I knew from the initial email that Jennifer was a serious, intelligent person. Her resume was so good it almost didn't seem real. In addition to her counter intelligence work, which included a stint at the Pentagon, she teaches forensic science and criminal justice at the American Military University. She served as a unit commander in South Korea and worked in the New York City Medical Examiner's Office for more than a year. Jennifer has multiple masters degrees and even worked a stint in the Arizona Department of Correction. She's also a licensed private investigator.

We began a correspondence. That first email led to hundreds of emails and text messages. Soon we were spending hours on the phone. One call lasted right at four hours. Jennifer wanted to write a series of stories for In Public Safety, a Web site sponsored by her university. She had written several articles about other murder cases, but this would be her most probative look into an unsolved murder.

At first, she thought a female or females killed Rebekah, just as I had speculated years earlier. The cleanup, lack of a sexual assault, and the fact that the police had seemingly cleared McCullough. As her researched deepened, her opinions changed, and her work added dramatic new layers to the known evidence.

Jennifer has a unique ability to focus on a detail, however minor, and stay with it until a satisfactory explanation is reached. For example, one of the first things we discussed was whether there was one blow or two. The autopsy said it could be either, and I tended to think it was just one.

She and her husband, Jesse, had a hard time believing it was a piano leg and did experiments with various types of objects such as the butt of a gun to determine what kind of damage would be caused. To complete her work, she needed the autopsy report, and I thought that Larry would be glad to give it to her. Less than a month later, she and her husband left their Colorado Springs home and came to Arkansas.

I arranged a meeting with Larry and Danielle. We met at Larry's house and talked for several hours. Jennifer told me during this meeting she was now sure it was a love interest that killed Rebekah in a rage-fueled fit. She spent several days in Arkansas, retracing the steps the killer took in the moments after the murder. With copies of the autopsy and the independent analysis in hand, she went home and started an even deeper dive.

With the help of a friend who is a nurse and skilled in head trauma, she determined there was a direct blow to the front of the face on the left side, and a second blow to the left side of the cranium. Her analysis was incredible. I now believe the killer wielded two blows.

Another detail she spent a lot of time examining was the route the killer took to dispose of the body, and the psychological markers that could be gleaned from the act. As was mentioned before, a gravel road connects the highway near McCullough's house to the very spot where Rebekah was found. In fact, the little used roadway ends very near the dumpsite.

The killer, Jennifer speculated, had to dispose of her there because it was the end of the road, and he would have to drive onto the main road, Arkansas 9, and didn't want to have the body in his vehicle. The place chosen also offered other clues about the killer. It was likely not a route the killer would have to pass on his way to go to work or take part in normal life activities.

There would be an enormous mental toll the killer would have to deal with each time he passed that spot. The dumpsite is not well known, meaning the killer had to live in the general area. She was likely laid in the spot where she was found, not tossed down the embankment.

Another area that Jennifer deep dove into was the time of death. The autopsy report didn't state what types of maggots were found on Rebekah, but the largest measured about half an inch, according to the report. It takes about 12 to 24 hours for maggot activity to begin after death. The size of the maggots indicated activity had started roughly 6.25 days from the time she was found. Add in the hours it took for the activity to start after death, and Jennifer was able to deduce Rebekah likely died before noon on Sept. 20, 2004.

Of all the things we discussed, and all the things she wrote about, one detail emerged that caught everyone's attention. In several news articles, the responding officer, Charlie Melton said he opened the lid of the washing machine during the wellness check and discovered the bloody sheets. Jennifer spun on this for more than a month.

"Why would he check the washing machine?" she asked me. "A human body wouldn't fit in there, so why check there?"

I told her that may be he noticed the sheets were off the bed and it was a natural response to look for them. She said that was possible, but then asked the follow up question.

She had another explanation. Jennifer thinks the washing machine was still running when Melton walked into the house. He stated previously that the agitator had blood in it. The only way that's possible is if it was still cycling of if the person that placed the sheets in there turned it off mid-cycle and left it there. If the cycle had been completed the blood and water would have been gone.

Melton could easily clear this topic, but when Jennifer tried to contact him he hung the phone up on her. I thought was extremely unprofessional, and it's a subject he's openly discussed with reporters in years past, so I don't know why he wouldn't talk with Jennifer. I've been told he's relayed to others the machine wasn't on, but it's still a murky point until he publicly says so.

There were other clues that Jennifer was able to glean even without the case file. For starters, there's no DNA or forensic evidence (such as fingerprints) that ties these other suspects to the crime scene. If they had recovered this evidence, than there would have been arrested or at the very least be named as a suspect. Jennifer thinks the house was covered with Casey and Rebekah's DNA and fingerprints. It's unlikely a killer that did such a clumsy cleanup job when taken in totality would have brought gloves along.

Jennifer did something I should have done years ago in her eighth article. She created a criteria that only the killer could meet. The person who killed Rebekah Gould fits most, if not all, of this criteria Jennifer created:

An alibi that is impossible to prove;

Admitted that he was at Casey's house on Tuesday morning;

DNA and fingerprints that would not look out of place in Casey's house;

A history of a personal and intimate relationship with Rebekah;

A history of violent outbursts;

Access to a vehicle;

Knowledge of the local area;

A first-hand changing timeline of events;

An inability (i.e., refusal) to remember key pieces of the timeline prior to Rebekah's murder;

Access to Casey's house and backyard, on two different days, without looking out of place;

A lack of interest in searching for Rebekah's body or attending her funeral;

Knowledge of the loose piano leg if it was used as the murder weapon;

Familiarity with both Rebekah's and Casey's dogs;

A refusal to discuss his theory on what happened to Rebekah;

Trust from Rebekah for her to remain in her underwear in his presence;

Lived in the area.

This criteria virtually eliminates nearly all the other speculated suspects. In Jennifer's version of events, the killer did a rudimentary cleanup in the moments after the killing. It would have taken about 15 minutes of less to drive from Casey's house to the dumpsite. The killer had an obligation, such as work, that had to be met. He intended to return later to finish the cleanup and dispose of Rebekah's belongings. Jennifer believes the killer returned Tuesday morning to finish the cleanup. That would explain why the towels were in the dryer and the sheets were in the washer.

In addition to this list, Jennifer included several provocative questions in her story. "Why move the body?" "Who has the overwhelming motive to remove Rebekah's body and clean the crime scene?" "Who would feel comfortable returning to the scene of the crime to conduct a further cleanup and why do it at all?"

That criteria and those questions clearly speak for themselves. Jennifer's work on this case has been powerful and I'm very grateful she's gotten involved. Prosecutors and police have not been forthcoming with her, but I hope that changes. She was slated to meet with Larry and Arkansas Lt. Gov. Tim Griffin in late April, 2019.

Jennifer and I made a deal that we will sit together in the court room when Rebekah's killer is arraigned in open court. It's a deal I hope we get to complete.

This is what I think happened.

Rebekah dropped McCullough off at work that morning with the understanding that their relationship was coming to an end. She stopped at the store and bought the breakfast sandwich. She went back to his house to take a nap. She was in her t-shirt and panties, and that's how she slept, Danielle told me. There was a coffee cup in the microwave and an uneaten breakfast sandwich still in the house. She was supposed to pick Danielle up around noon, and Rebekah had a habit of napping in the morning, Danielle said.

"Everything about it ... was just so Rebekah. That was Rebekah," Danielle told me.

Rebekah was in a remote trailer house, down a desolate road. Her killer had to know she was at the house, and it's almost certain she knew this person. If it were a stranger, she would have fought her attacker off, and if she were asleep, her dog would have alerted her. There would have been defensive wounds.

This was a rage killing. The murderer struck her with enough force to kill her in one or two blows. She died on or very near the bed in the bedroom. Most of the blood was found in the bedroom on the bed, baseboards, and walls. The bloody sheets were in the washing machine. I am told the top section of the bed was cut away and taken as evidence. That means she bled a lot on that bed.

Rebekah could have been laying on her side, asleep when the blow was delivered. It's also possible she may have gotten into an argument with her killer, turned her head slightly and never saw the lethal hit coming, and that could explain the lack of defensive wounds.

As far as the killer goes, it was someone she knew and someone her dog knew. This person had to know about the piano leg. This person obviously felt comfortable in the house. The killer went to great lengths to clean up the blood splatter and tried to conceal where she died by flipping the mattress and washing the sheets. Bloody pillows were placed underneath the bed. The responding officer, Melton, noted that when he first went into the house nothing seemed to be amiss. This speaks to how much time and effort the killer put into the cleanup.

There are still significant questions that relate to the killer. Why move her body? Why clean? Why do all of that and leave her car, purse, keys, cell phone, clothes, and dog? It's almost as if the killer just didn't have enough time to remove all the evidence, but why remove any of it at all?

Everything in this case points to the killer being a love interest. If there is video of McCullough at work all day, then the police should release the video. It would clear his name, and that would be a major benefit to him, his family, and the community. Any notion that releasing that video would impair the investigation is hogwash. Releasing a video of an innocent person at work would do nothing to impair the investigation. I think that every single person following this case on either side of this debate would agree the video needs to be released.

More positive news poured in during the spring of 2019. The Vidocq Society, an organization that helps to solve cold case murders agreed to examine the case. Its membership includes a wide array of law enforcement officials from around the country. Jim Fitzgerald, an FBI profiler who helped to find the Unabomber is a member and has studied aspects of this case.

The family's one singular goal throughout all of these years is justice for Rebekah.

"We need to get justice for her ... she didn't get to meet my girls," Danielle said of her own two daughters. "She didn't get to be a mom. She needs justice."

Hearing those words from Danielle reminded of the saddest line I read on Rebekah's death certificate. On the certificate, it states the day and manner in which she lost her life. It states where it happened and lists her home address – McCullough's house. Under marital status, there are two words, which demonstrate something else that was stolen from this young woman. The words put a lump in my throat every time I read them.

"Never married."

Actor Johnny Depp and former Death Row prisoner Damien Echols attended a rally to in Little Rock days before Arkansas started the planned executions of eight Death Row inmates in April 2017. Photo/Jared.

From left to right: Death Row inmates Kenneth Williams, Jack Jones Jr., Ledell Lee, and Marcel Williams.

From left to bottom: Estelle Laughlin and Henry Greenbaum with his wife.

From left, counter clockwise: Karen Johnson Swift, Rebekah Gould, and Amanda Tusing.

Made in United States
Orlando, FL
09 April 2022